Development and Utilisation of Water Supplies in the East Riding of Yorkshire

E. Aylwin and R. C. Ward

University of Hull
Occasional Papers in Geography No. 10

Development and Utilisation of Water Supplies in the East Riding of Yorkshire

University of Hull Publications

Occasional Papers in Geography No. 10

General Editor: H. R. Wilkinson

Professor of Geography in the University of Hull

DEVELOPMENT AND UTILISATION OF WATER SUPPLIES IN THE EAST RIDING OF YORKSHIRE

E. AYLWIN
and
R. C. WARD

University of Hull
1969

SBN 90048020-3

Made and Printed in England
by Hull Printers Limited
Great Gutter Lane, Willerby, Hull, Yorkshire

CONTENTS

ABBREVIATIONS USED IN TEXT

E.R.C.C.	East Riding County Council
EY (WA) WB	East Yorkshire (Wolds Area) Water Board
g.p.d.	gallons per day
g.p.h.	gallons per hour
g.p.h.p.d.	gallons per head per day
H.E.Y.R.B.	Hull and East Yorkshire River Board
M.A.F.F.	Ministry of Agriculture, Food and Fisheries
M.B.	Municipal Borough
m.g.a.	million gallons per annum
m.g.d.	million gallons per day
R.D.	Rural District
R.D.C.	Rural District Council
R.J.W.B.	Ryedale Joint Water Board
U.D.	Urban District
U.D.C.	Urban District Council
Y.O.H.R.A.	Yorkshire Ouse and Hull River Authority
Y.O.R.B.	Yorkshire Ouse River Board

FIGURES

PLATES

TABLES

PREFACE AND ACKNOWLEDGEMENTS

The British Isles are, in general, well endowed with water but because of local inequalities in the distribution of supply and demand, water shortages have been for many years a constant threat, and in many cases, an uncomfortable reality. Growing interest in, and concern about, the nation's water supplies culminated, in 1963, in the Water Resources Act, which represents the most comprehensive attempt to date to provide for the planned conservation and exploitation of water in England and Wales. The old River Boards were swept away and upon the new River Authorities was laid a statutory obligation to measure the water resources actually available to them. This has, in most cases, involved the establishment of hydrometric schemes to measure rainfall, evaporation, soil moisture, groundwater and streamflow.

Concomitant with the progress embodied in the 1963 Act and in earlier water resource legislation in 1945 and 1948, there was a growing, voluntarily undertaken, rationalisation within the water industry itself, which resulted in a considerable reduction in the multiplicity of water undertakings from 1,226 in 1956 to 335 in 1966. Logically, the next step, which has already been envisaged by some of the industry's more forward thinkers, is a formal association between the River Authorities and the water undertakings, so that those responsible for controlling water resources and those responsible for the distribution of water supplies, are working on the same side of the fence.

It is against this background of an increasing impetus towards change that the following paper must be read. From this point of view, the East Riding of Yorkshire provides an admirable study area, for there has been not only an amalgamation of the former Yorkshire Ouse River Board and the Hull and East Yorkshire River Board to form the Yorkshire Ouse and Hull River Authority, but also an extensive rationalisation of the water supply industry, particularly in recent years, so that by the end of 1963, only three undertakings were using East Riding water sources, compared with the total for four years earlier of 17.

Grateful thanks are extended to W. F. Gilbert, Esq., M. A. (Oxon.), M.I.C.E., M.I.W.E., Engineer to the former Hull and East Yorkshire River Board (and now Engineer to the Yorkshire Ouse and Hull River Authority) and his staff, and to T. G. S. Green, Esq., M.Sc., A.M.I.C.E., of the former Yorkshire Ouse River Board, for a great deal of information which was always very willingly supplied; to the Clerks, Engineers and Surveyors of each statutory water supply undertaking in the East Riding who made water supply data freely available for consultation; to the staff in the Beverley office of the Ministry of Agriculture, Fisheries and Food and farmers visited; to the County Archivist and to the Consulting Engineers A. C. Fairbank, Esq., M.I.C.E., M.I.W.E., M.Cons.E., at York; J. H. Haiste, Esq., M.I.C.E., M.I.W.E., M.Cons.E., M.I.Mech.E., at Leeds; and D. H. Moore, Esq., B.Sc., M.I.C.E., at Scarborough, for invaluable historical information; and to J. R. A. Garland, Esq., M.I.C.E., M.I.W.E., Engineer to the former West Sussex River Board (and now Chief Engineer to the Sussex River Authority) for his encouragement in this investigation.

The authors are also grateful to Mrs. J. Dealtry and Miss P. A. Ashcroft for typing most of the manuscript, to Mr. R. R. Dean and his staff in the Drawing Office for work on the line illustrations and to Mr. J. B. Fisher in the Photographic Laboratory for his work on the plates.

E. Aylwin
R. C. Ward

Department of Geography,
University of Hull.

June, 1968.

CHAPTER 1

INTRODUCTION AND PHYSICAL BACKGROUND

THE smallest of the three Ridings in Yorkshire, the administrative county of the East Riding has an area of 1,176 square miles. It is 42 miles wide from Cawood in the west to Aldbrough in the east, and 33 miles from north to south between Filey and Hull. Population at the 1961 Census was 527,292, representing

TABLE 1

Yorkshire, East Riding	525,300
Kingston upon Hull M.B.	300,790
Administrative County	224,510
Municipal Boroughs and Urban Districts	112,900
Beverley M.B.	15,890
Bridlington M.B.	25,590
Driffield U.D.	6,820
Filey U.D.	4,500
Haltemprice U.D.	42,330
Hedon M.B.	2,340
Hornsea U.D.	5,750
Norton U.D.	4,840
Withernsea U.D.	4,840
Rural Districts	111,610
Beverley	23,650
Bridlington	9,230
Derwent	13,760
Driffield	11,330
Holderness	20,370
Howden	12,070
Norton	7,050
Pocklington	14,150

POPULATION IN THE EAST RIDING, 1961
Source:— Registrar-General (1964)

an increase of 16,388 over the 1951 Census, with the greatest increase in Haltemprice U.D. Table 1 illustrates the dominance of Kingston upon Hull over the county. Apart from Hull there are almost equal numbers of people in rural districts and urban areas in the rest of the East Riding. Agriculture is the basis of the county's economy and, if the population of Hull is excluded, provides employment for one-fifth of the male population in the East Riding. (Board of Trade, 1958). Most of the industrial development is in Hull and its immediate hinterland, though some smaller firms operate in the market towns of Howden, Pocklington, Norton, Driffield and Beverley, and the seaside towns of Filey, Bridlington, Hornsea and Withernsea.

The Rivers Derwent, Ouse and Humber form geographical as well as administrative boundaries on the north, west and south respectively, while the North Sea forms the eastern boundary. Purely administrative boundaries are those between York and Stamford Bridge, and between Binnington Carr and North Cliff in the north-west and north-east of the county respectively.

The upland area of the Wolds can be seen in Figure 1 (*a*) to sweep round in a wide arc from the chalk cliffs of Flamborough Head to the Humber, reaching its highest point near Garrowby Hill (808 ft. O.D.) but decreasing in height to 400 ft O.D. nearer the Humber in the south. The chalk of the Wolds presents a steep scarp face to the Vales of Pickering and York, but dips gently eastwards and south-eastwards where it is covered by the Pleistocene deposits of the Plain of Holderness. The range of altitude in these lowland areas is small. The Vale of Pickering varies in height between 65 and 100 ft O.D., the Vale of York is largely below 50 ft O.D., and much of it lies below 25 ft O.D., while the Plain of Holderness exceeds 50 feet O.D. only in the east.

The relationship of these four geomorphological regions to the underlying geology is evident in Figure 1 (*b*). The Keuper Marl and Bunter Sandstone of the Trias form the floor of the Vale of York. The Jurassic shales, sandstones and limestones outcrop in the eastern part of the Howardian Hills, south of Norton, but also form a narrow outcrop at the foot of the western escarpment of the Wolds, only two miles wide at its widest outcrop.The Cretaceous Wolds cross earlier strata with a well-marked unconformity, and Versey (1948) described the structure as a syncline trending from north-west to south-east.

The importance of the chalk as the major aquifer (the sands and gravel as a minor one) and the relative unimportance of the Jurassic and Triassic strata in relation to underground water resources in the county can be judged from the calculations of Fox-Strangways

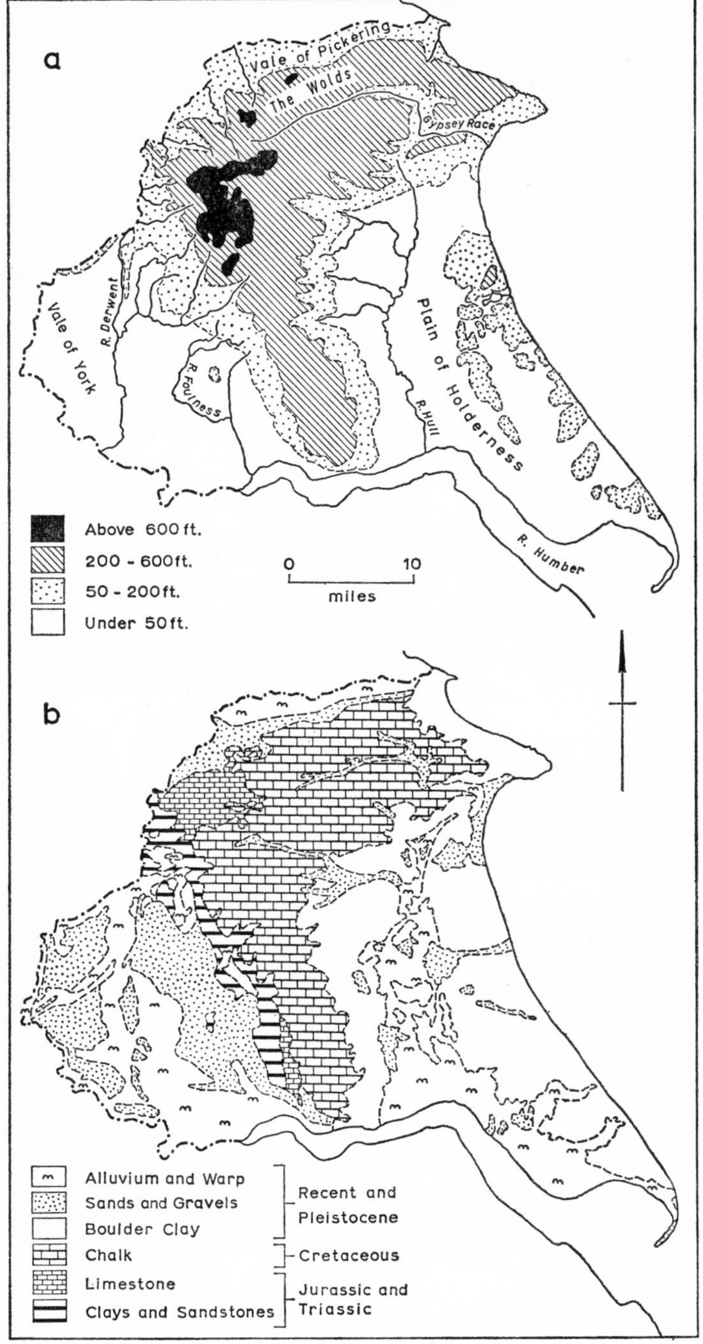

FIG. 1. SIMPLIFIED MAPS OF (*a*) RELIEF AND MAIN RIVERS and (*b*) GEOLOGY.

(1906) shown in Table 2. The pervious and partially pervious formations occupy about two-fifths, and the mainly impervious deposits, of which the Boulder Clay and, to a lesser extent, the alluvium are the most important deposits, occupy about three-fifths of the total area of the county.

TABLE 2

Geological Deposit	Area of pervious and partially pervious deposits (square miles)	Area of mainly impervious deposits (square miles)	Percentage of total area of County
Gravels of dry valleys	5	—	—
Alluvium, mainly warp clay	—	267	23
Sands and gravel	153	—	13
Boulder clay	—	356	30
Glacial sands and gravel	33	—	4
Chalk	294	—	25
Lower Cretaceous, Kimmeridge, Oxford } Clays	—	13	1
Middle Oolites	8	—	} 1
Lower Oolites	7	—	
Lias	—	24	2
Keuper Marl	—	14	1
	500	674	100
Percentage of total area of County	42·59	57·41	100

AREAS OF PERVIOUS AND IMPERVIOUS DEPOSITS

Source: Memoir of the Geological Survey, 1906.

The Bunter Sandstones on the western side of the River Ouse provide potable water supplies for Selby and Goole, both of which supply the south-western part of the East Riding. Although these Triassic rocks have small outcrop, they have a high porosity and permeability, and relatively high specific yield, so that they can provide satisfactory sources of water, particularly where water can percolate readily through the overlying Pleistocene deposits. It has, in fact been shown that the quality of Triassic ground water deteriorates eastwards from the River Ouse towards the Wolds as the Drift cover increases in depth (Lapworth, 1933) thereby reducing the circulation of water underground, as also happens in the Plain of Holderness. This factor precludes the use of ground-water for potable supplies between Selby and the springs issuing from the foot of the western escarpment of the Wolds. Furthermore, the Triassic water in the vicinity of York is very hard and, though suitable for brewing, is unsuitable for drinking, so that York Water Company abstracts water from the River Ouse at Acomb.

The superficial deposits overlying the Jurassic rocks in the Vale of Pickering consist of the main deposits of the post-glacial Lake Pickering together with sands and gravels, including blown sand. A layer of gravel below the clay and peat of the main lake deposits produces an artesian supply south of the River Derwent whose source according to Versey (1949) is water percolating from the chalk, since the percolation of water in the low-lying vale itself could not develop sufficient head to produce an artesian supply.

The Plain of Holderness consists of a series of glacial drifts lying on the buried chalk surface. The drift cover increases south-eastwards from approximately 35 feet at Beverley and Cottingham to 160 feet at Patrington, and eastwards to approximately 85 feet at Brandesburton and between 135 and 140 feet at Hornsea (Silcock, 1922). As in the Vale of York, water obtained from boreholes increases in hardness towards the coast as the Boulder Clay increases in thickness, and it becomes increasingly ferruginous. Small quantities of water are still obtained from aquifers of gravel in the Boulder Clay, but are liable to pollution. Oakley, Bush and Toombs (1944) for example, described wells at Burshill and Routh where the supply was ferruginous and contaminated. Reid (1885) described the springs which rise through the drift of Holderness along its western edge known locally as 'Kells' or 'Kelds'. Many of these springs, including Keldgate Spring, flowed in December 1960 and January 1961, for the first time in many years when artesian conditions existed for a distance of 1½ miles in Cottingham village.

Only where the Howardian Hills extend eastward into the East Riding is the outcrop of the Corallian rocks of the Jurassic sufficiently extensive to form an important aquifer, e.g. boreholes at Howe Hill supply Norton with water. The outcrop almost disappears on the northern side of the Market Weighton anticlinorium, and south of this is only wide enough to supply small springs.

It is the chalk of the Wolds, 1,500 feet thick at its maximum and with an average thickness of 900 feet along the western margin of Holderness, which forms the major aquifer. The main groundwater supplies are drawn from the region floored by Upper Chalk but there is little lithological difference between the Middle and Upper chalk in the county, apart from an absence of flints in the Upper Chalk. Versey (1949), in fact, considered the chalk as one large aquifer, since the porosity of the Lower Chalk differs very little from that of the other two divisions, although local variations may occur where marl bands occasionally produce small perched water tables. The main flow of water is through joints and fissures so that when a new underground water supply source is developed, adits are driven from the boreholes at right angles to the flow of water, in order to intersect as many fissures as possible. Versey (1949) described the variability of frequency of joints in the Wolds with a north-west to south-east direction and associated direction of water movement between Bridlington and Driffield, and a north-east to south-west direction carrying the flow in the same direction in the southern area.

The intermittent stream called the Gypsey Race, whose maximum length is shown in Figure 1 (*a*), forms the only surface drainage on the Wolds. It follows the broad Great Wold Valley which has a west-east trend in the northern Wolds. The valley is deflected southwards by the Hunmanby fault, to Rudston, whence it resumes its west-east trend, and the Gypsey Race flows into the North Sea in Bridlington Harbour.

The present surface drainage of the three lowland areas began to develop as the ice retreated at the end of the last glaciation. The River Hull is fed by springs from the dip-slope of the Wolds and by westward-flowing streams rising from the drift deposits in the Plain of Holderness to the east. The effect of the spring discharges forming the West Beck tributary of the River Hull is generally to cause a steady increase in the flow from November or early December. The flow reaches a maximum in February when the water table is at its highest and ground water storage at a maximum, then decreases steadily to a minimum in June or July. This regime will alter with any appreciable variation in the incidence of rainfall, particularly in September and October when the water table is beginning to rise. The River Hull has a very flat gradient, falling only seven feet in 22 miles between Emmotland and the Humber, and it is tidal up to the sluice gates at Tophill Low Pumping Station. No drainage works were carried out in the peat lands of the River Hull valley and Holderness Carrs until the eighteenth and nineteenth centuries, although the silt lands near the mouth of the river were drained earlier into the River Humber.

In the Vale of York the River Derwent extends south from the Kirkham Gorge overflow channel towards the River Ouse. It is joined by spring-fed streams rising at the foot of the western escarpment of the Wolds in the Pocklington area. Similar spring-fed streams in the Market Weighton area join to form the River Foulness which flows westwards and then turns south and east to enter the Wallingfen depression which is followed by the Market Weighton canal.

The River Derwent rises six miles from the North Sea in Fylingdales Moor and discharges into the River Ouse at Barmby on the Marsh, 58 miles west of the North Sea at Spurn Head. Apart from a limited volume discharged into the North Sea at Scalby during flood times down the artificial channel called the Sea Cut, the entire run-off from a watershed of 757 square miles is evacuated by the River Derwent into the Ouse. Below Elvington weir, the river is tidal for the remaining 16 miles to its confluence with the River Ouse, and, like the River Hull, it has a very flat gradient in this tidal length. The channel has been widened, deepened, and in places straightened to alleviate flooding, and as in the cases of the Rivers Hull and Ouse it is confined within artificially raised embankments. The rivers can, therefore, accommodate medium floods but maximum floods still over-top embankments and flood the adjacent washlands.

The River Ouse is tidal downstream from Naburn Locks (south of York). The River Ouse, below its confluence with the River Trent at Trent Falls, becomes the River Humber which drains an area of over 10,000 square miles. The Humber estuary extends for a distance of 20 miles eastwards, and then a further 20 miles south-eastwards to Spurn Head.

CHAPTER 2

THE DEVELOPMENT OF PUBLIC WATER SUPPLIES

INTRODUCTION

PARTLY because of the physical situation which has been discussed in Chapter I and partly because of the historical growth and development of the area, there has emerged a strong contrast between the scale of public water supplies in Hull and that of the undertakings in the East Riding itself. For convenience, therefore, the development of public water supplies in the East Riding and in Hull will be considered separately, and in that order, in the following discussion. It is felt that this will in no way mask, and may, in some respects, help to emphasise the growing domination and influence of Hull on the public water supplies of adjacent areas of the County.

The absence of surface water, apart from the intermittent Gypsey Race, on the Wolds of East Yorkshire, has always proved a major obstacle to settlement and has been largely responsible for the low density of population in this part of the County. It is not unnatural, therefore, that the area's earliest recorded water supplies were located in the Wolds. These were ponds at places such as Sledmere, Wetwang and Wharram Percy, some dating from as early as 1303 (Cole, 1894). In the eighteenth century Leatham (1794) described circular ponds on the Wolds, particularly in the higher parts where a water supply was required for stock, and Marshall (1796) reported more general use of cistern-stored rain water for human consumption. He also described the construction of circular ponds for field water supplies, which were usually from 18 to 20 yards in diameter. He noted that ". . . while one man was driving his flock, three or four miles to water, his neighbours, who had made ponds upon their farms, were free from this serious inconveniency".

Harris (1961) described the new farm houses appearing in the late eighteenth and early nineteenth centuries on the outer fringes of the newly inclosed villages, so that the village pond was more distant for them. However, in Young's writings, the dryness of the

Wolds is dismissed as being ". . . not insurmountable; for wells have been sunk with success in the very highest places: scarce a village on the Wolds is without a pond at least, which furnishes a supply for cattle, and every other purpose, except drink for the inhabitants". (Young, 1770). The population of the Wolds increased in the early nineteenth century but an agricultural depression at this time produced some emigration, as from Helperthorpe in the Great Wold Valley, for example, between 1841 and 1851 (Harris, 1961).

At least 9 wells, of which details are given in Table 3, had been sunk in the Wolds before 1855. All these early Wold wells, except that at Hunmanby, formed the domestic water supply for the villages shown and were usually fitted with pumps. Many of these village pumps, though long since disused still exist beside the church or village green (Plate I).

TABLE 3

Region	Site	Date	Depth in Feet	Geology	Water Supply
Vale of York	(1) Stamford Bridge	C. 1840	120	Trias	Domestic
	(2) Holme on Spalding Moor	Before 1853	24	Sandstone Drift	Domestic
	(3) Youlthorpe	Before 1855	59	Keuper Marl	Farm
Northern Wolds	(4) Hunmanby	Before 1855	80	Chalk	Farm
	(5) Butterwick	Before 1855	120	Chalk	Public Pump
	(6) Foxholes	Before 1855	84	Chalk	Public Pump
	(7) Thwing	Before 1855	250	Chalk	Public Pump
	(8) West Lutton	Before 1855	66	Chalk	Public Pump
	(9) Langtoft	Before 1855	C.126	Chalk	Public Pump
	(10) Sledmere	Before 1855	182	Chalk	Public Pump
Central Wolds	(11) Middleton-on-the-Wolds	Before 1855	71	Chalk	Public Pump
Southern Wolds	(12) Skidby	Before 1855	10	Sand	Public Pump

DETAILS OF WELLS SUNK BEFORE 1855

Source: Oakley and others, 1944.

In contrast to the dryness of the Wolds, the surrounding clay lowlands of Holderness and the Vale of York were, paradoxically, too wet, so that settlements tended to be mainly located either at the junction with the Wolds or on local patches of higher, or better drained land. Certainly, before the beginning of the eighteenth century, villages in the Vale of York were small and were scattered along the banks of the Rivers Ouse and Derwent, and along the scarp foot spring line of the Wolds. York, Malton and Selby provided the market centres but were all outside the county boundary. Harris (1961) described the larger centres of population of Pocklington, the parish and town of Howden, and the parish of Hemingbrough as having 235, 350 and 300 families respectively in 1743. In the first half of the nineteenth century the small market towns of Howden, Market Weighton and Pocklington grew until, by 1851, the population of each exceeded 2000. Again, due to poor drainage in the carr and silt lands of Holderness and the River Hull valley the population was scattered in small villages on higher mounds of Boulder Clay, sands and gravel where some source of drinking water could be obtained from shallow wells. Apart from Hull, the largest settlements in 1743 were the market towns of Beverley and Bridlington, with 550 and 527 families respectively, and the ancient borough of Hedon and the village of Patrington with 100 families each. The town of Beverley was typical of these larger settlements in having a supply of water in the streets by the eighteenth century from several pumped wells, although some trouble was experienced with pollution and the Corporation were forced to take measures to prevent new pumps being used for watering horses and cattle (MacMahon, 1958).

A hand pump over a spring formed the first recorded public water supply in Bridlington, in 1811, when the population had reached 3,741. For those who did not wish to visit the pump, on the slipway between Princes Street and the harbour, water was sold around the streets from a mobile barrel at ½*d.* or 1*d.* per bucket.

Clearly all the water supply sources mentioned previously were liable to pollution, for, as Table 3 shows, most of the early wells were fairly shallow and farm cisterns were often contaminated from sewage-soaked soil. Pollution of water supplies was particularly bad in the Vale of York, where shallow wells with loose brick linings, and cisterns and brick ponds of shallow water formed the

I. Public Pump, West End, Kilha

II. Marl Pond near Harswel

three main sources of supply. Plate II shows one of these ponds between Holme-on-Spalding-Moor and Harswell, in mid-summer when the water was stagnant; this is typical of many such pools at Blacktoft, Broomfleet, Cotness, Faxfleet and elsewhere.

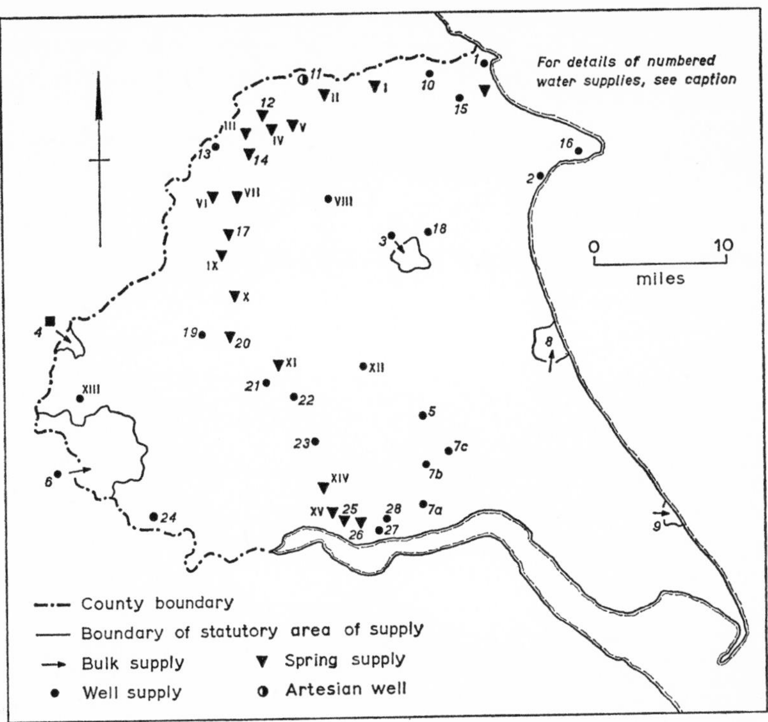

FIG. 2. STATUTORY WATER SUPPLY UNDERTAKINGS, 1933.
Based on data in Lapworth (1933). Numbered supplies areas as follows: 1–9 Large public water supply undertakings (i.e. 1. Filey U.D.C., 2. Bridlington Corporation, 3. Driffield Water Co., 4. York Water Co., 5. Beverley Corporation, 6. Selby U.D., 7. Kingston upon Hull Corporation, 8 Hornsea U.D.C., 9. Withernsea U.D.C.); 10–28 Small public water supply undertakings (i.e. 10. Folkton. 11. Yedingham, 12. Rillington, 13. Norton U.D.C., 14. Settrington, 15. Hunmanby, 16. Flamborough, 17. Thixendale, 18. Nafferton, 19. Barmby on the Moor, 20. Pocklington Water Co., 21. Shiptonthorpe, 22. Market Weighton Water Co., 23. South Newbald, 24. Asselby, 25. Elloughton and Brough Water Co., 26. Welton, 27. North Ferriby, 28. Swanland); i–xv Estate supplies (i.e., i. Ganton, ii. East Heslerton, iii. Scagglethorpe, iv. Thorpe Bassett, v. Wintringham, vi. Burythorpe, vii. Birdsall Estate, viii. Sledmere Estate, ix. Kirby Underdale with Garrowby, x. Great Givendale with Grimthorpe, xi. Londesborough with Easthorpe, xii. Dalton Estate, xiii. Escrick Park Estate, xiv. South Cave Water Co., xv. Brantingham).

After 1855 deeper wells were sunk by specialised firms, and in the latter part of the nineteenth century the Railway Companies started to sink wells for domestic supplies at new stations, and owners of private estates began to supply piped water to their employees, as well as to their own residences. The Sykes family at Sledmere Hall, for example, had a well dug before 1855, from which water was pumped to two reservoirs on high ground behind the village before flowing back by gravity to standpipes in the village street, where a pure water supply could be obtained by estate workers. There were fifteen private estate and village supplies in the county by 1933 (see Fig. 2) although the date of installation of these is unknown, apart from that of the South Cave Water Company's supply in about 1872 and the Escrick Park Estate supply in 1890.

TABLE 4

Date of Census	Population	Intercensal Increase	
		Amount	Per Cent Per Year
1801 March 9/10	110,614		
1811 May 26/27	133,209	22,595	1·84
1821 May 27/28	153,912	20,703	1·45
1831 May 29/30	168,075	14,163	0·88
1841 June 6/7	193,792	25,717	1·43
1851 March 30/31	219,235	25,443	1·26
1861 April 7/8	238,034	18,799	0·82
1871 April 2/3	265,295	27,261	1·09
1881 April 3/4	309,408	44,113	1·55
1891 April 5/6	341,546	32,138	0·99
1901 March 31/April 1	385,007	43,447	1·21
1911 April 2/3	432,759	47,752	1·18
1921 June 19/20	460,880	28,121	0·62
1931 April 26/27	482,936	22,056	0·48
1939 Mid-year estimate	505,980	23,044	0·57
1951 April 8/9	510,904	4,924	0·08
1961 April 23/24	527,292	16,388	0·31

POPULATION INCREASE IN THE EAST RIDING, 1801-1961 (1801-1891 ANCIENT COUNTY; FROM 1891 ADMINISTRATIVE COUNTY WITH ASSOCIATED C.B.)

In the latter half of the nineteenth century, with increasing population and increasing pollution of water supplies, prominent citizens formed Water Committees in the larger towns and eventually obtained the necessary legislation to form Water Companies. The steady increase in population in the county, including Hull, between 1801 and 1961 is summarized in Table 4.

The population in the rural districts was almost stationary between 1911 and 1931 and it can be seen in Figure 3 that the largest increases in the first half of the twentieth century were in

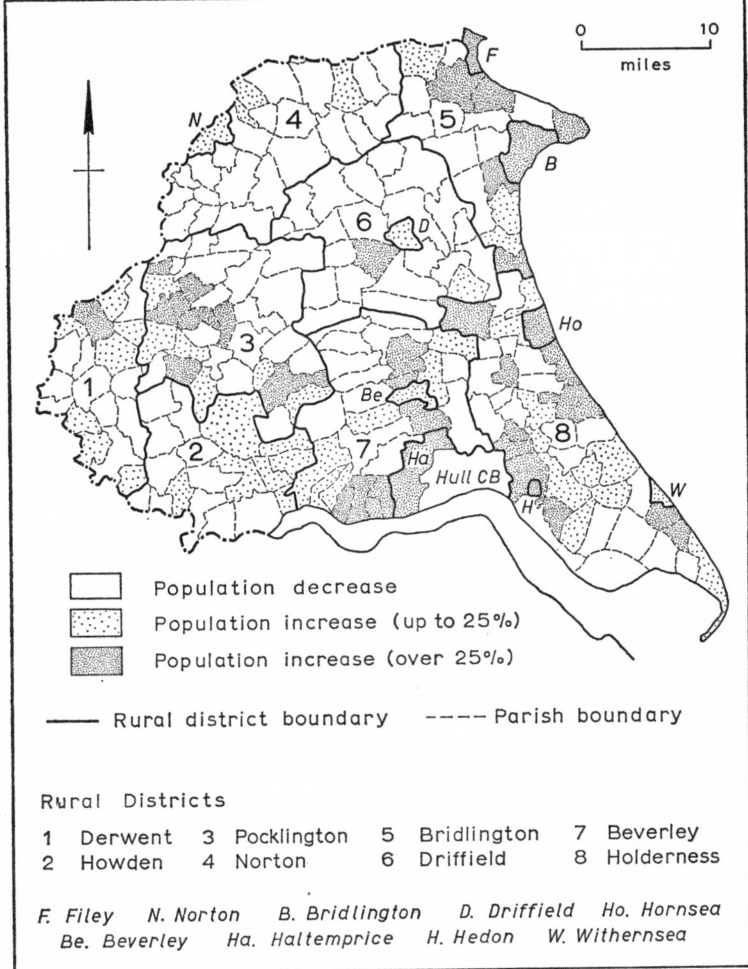

FIG. 3. ESTIMATED POPULATION CHANGES, 1921–49
Based on a map in East Riding County Council. (1952).

parishes adjacent to the coastal resorts of Filey, Bridlington, Hornsea and Withernsea, and in Haltemprice, in the parishes adjacent to Hull. The decline in population in many of the Wolds parishes, and in several parishes in the centre of the Vale of York, is very apparent, the most significant decreases occurring in the Rural Districts of Norton and Driffield, where many Wolds parishes are served only by minor roads.

Piped water supplies were extended in rural areas following the Rural Water Supplies Act, 1934. Most Rural Districts prepared 'regional schemes' and received Government grants towards the cost of mains networks and the development of new sources of supply. More remote farms received piped supplies after the passing of the Rural Water Supplies and Sewerage Act of 1944, under which the Rural Districts could apply for Exchequer and County Council grants-in-aid for mains extensions and other works.

THE WATER COMPANIES AND STATUTORY UNDERTAKINGS

Filey

The population of Filey in 1856 was 2,000 in the summer and 1,500 in the winter, living in 393 houses. When the Filey Waterworks Company was inaugurated, on 1st August of the same year, the town already contained 64 lodgings, six inns and three hotels, and obtained its water supplies from 57 private and two public wells. However, all the private wells had been condemned and most of them dried up in the summer months. In 1857, the Waterworks Company completed an open reservoir fed by spring water, at Rosedale, south of Filey (Plate III), together with a filter bed and five miles of mains, making it possible to supply 100 houses and some shops in the town. The Water Company purchased the Gas Company in 1859 forming the Filey Water and Gas Company, which supplied 250 consumers in 1860. By 1885 the winter population had increased to 2,200 and the supply from Rosedale reservoir was proving inadequate, and causing complaints by 1890, despite the construction of a covered reservoir at Rosedale in 1887. Accordingly, a 375-foot borehole was sunk in 1890, a reservoir was constructed at

Station Avenue and the water was fed into the town's mains. The spring yield at Rosedale reservoirs, which was variable and becoming polluted, was no longer used after 1891. A water supply was provided for Gristhorpe village on 5th June, 1897, after the construction of new mains.

The Filey Water and Gas Act of 1st July, 1898, authorised Filey U.D.C. to supply water and gas and to acquire the Filey Water and Gas Company. The statutory area of supply was Filey and the parishes of Gristhorpe and Lebberston. The mains network was immediately improved and services extended, and in 1910 a new main was constructed between the Filey Pumping Station and Rosedale reservoirs, but again, by 1923, demand for water was increasing as the resort developed. A second borehole (425 feet) was sunk in 1925 at Station Avenue but proved a failure since the yield was only one-third that of borehole No. 1. However, in 1928 a third borehole (600 feet) was found to be successful and its output after chlorination and mixing with water from borehole No. 1 was pumped into the mains, any surplus water being pumped to the Rosedale reservoirs.

The increase in the number of consumers in Filey between 1928 and 1934, with the consequent increase in demand for water, can be seen in Table 5. Between 1928 and 1937 the number of consumers in Filey increased by 19% and the number of baths by 55%. In

TABLE 5

Year ending 31 March	1928	1929	1930	1931	1932	1933	1934
Number of consumers	1,269	1,292	1,303	1,380	1,423	1,457	1,477
Number of baths	559	603	693	723	741	745	796
Estimated permanent population					3,730	3,627	3,733
Estimated maximum population in holiday periods						8,000	8,200

INCREASE IN WATER CONSUMERS, FILEY, 1928-34

addition, parts of the parishes of Reighton and Hunmanby were transferred to Filey in 1935, and mains were laid in 1936 to Primrose Valley, south of Filey. In 1937 the 111 premises in Primrose Valley contained 107 baths and the estimated maximum population in the holiday period was 2,500. In 1939, in order to ensure maximum storage and maximum reliable yield, the northern reservoir at Rosedale was relined and new pumps were installed in boreholes No. 1 and No. 3.

During that year a winter population of 4,500, and a summer population of 8,500 to 10,000 were supplied with 24 g.p.h.p.d. By 1945, although the winter population had increased to only 5,000, the summer population was between 12,000 and 15,000 and Butlin's holiday village was growing rapidly, and in the following year the demand for water was 600,000 g.p.d. Accordingly, the southern reservoir at Rosedale was relined in 1946 and a new pump was installed in No. 1 borehole, and electricity was installed at Rosedale in 1947 so that modern booster pumping equipment could be used to maintain the supply to Butlin's camp and the Hunmanby Gap area. The supply at Rosedale was further improved in 1947 by the installation of two chlorinators and treatment plant.

The failure of the electric pump in No. 3 borehole during the 1952 holiday season resulted in complete loss of water supply to Butlin's camp and outlying farms at peak draw periods, and in order to prevent a recurrence of this situation, an 8-inch diameter main was constructed in 1954, providing a direct supply from the Rosedale reservoir to Butlin's camp. The Filey Water Order of 1953 empowered the construction of a new covered reservoir at Rosedale in order to eliminate contamination, a new borehole at Filey Pumping Station and an elevated tower at Mill Hill. This new source was urgently needed because in 1955 a further pump defect meant that total reliance was placed on one borehole source. The population in 1955 of 30,000 in Filey's statutory area of supply was made up as shown in Table 6.

TABLE 6

Location	Population
Filey Town	15,000
Butlin's Camp	8,000
Hunmanby Gap and Primrose Valley Caravan Sites and other 'holiday houses'	2,000
Camping Sites	5,000
TOTAL	30,000

FILEY, POPULATION COMPOSITION, 1955

Borehole No. 4, 600 feet deep and yielding 25,000 g.p.h., was completed at Station Road in 1957, the output being pumped into the mains and any surplus to Filey's requirements being pumped to the covered Rosedale reservoir. Such improvements resulted from the need to provide adequate water supplies at peak holiday periods for approximately six times the resident population. The water undertaking was superseded by the E.Y. (W.A.) W.B. on 1st April, 1962.

Bridlington

The Bridlington and Quay Water Company Ltd. provided the first piped water supply in Bridlington, in 1865, from a 6-ft diameter, 100 feet deep, chalk well at the junction of Marton Road and Mill Lane. The pumping station was constructed in 1865, with a small reservoir adjacent to it, and was called the Lower Works. Due to increasing demand for water from a growing residential population, and increasing popularity of the town as a seaside resort, the Higher Works were constructed in 1872 at the upper end of Mill Lane. These consisted of a 12-foot diameter, 160 feet deep chalk well, an engine and boiler house, an open reservoir and three houses for employees. The Company obtained powers, under the Bridlington Water Act (1895), to build a water tower for additional storage capacity.

In 1899 Bridlington U.D.C. purchased the Company and obtained powers under the Bridlington Water Order 1908, for new construction at the Higher Works. The second well was deepened to 193 feet in 1909, new boiler and engine houses were erected and new pumps and boilers installed. By 1912, 100 feet of adits had been driven from the well, and in 1925 the open reservoir was covered over to prevent pollution in summer. The new extensions were completed in 1933, with a new engine house containing diesel-engines and a new 24-inch diameter borehole. Increased housing development in the northern, higher part of the town necessitated the provision of increased storage capacity so that the Scarborough Road reservoir was constructed at 350 feet O.D. in 1933, two miles north of Mill Lane Pumping Station. This reservoir (Plate IV) was a conventional covered type of 50,000 gallon capacity, to which water was boosted from Mill Lane Pumping Station.

The increasing popularity of Bridlington as a seaside resort can be judged from the fact that between 1801 and 1931, the population increased from 3,130 to 20,194 and the number of inns, hotels and lodging houses increased from 69 in 1813 to 909 in 1913, all producing an ever-increasing demand for water, particularly in the summer months.

Flixton was the first village in Bridlington Rural District to have a piped water supply when, in 1900, a 5-foot diameter well was sunk 60 feet into the chalk. Water was originally wind-pumped into a 30,000 gallon reservoir at 260 feet O.D. In 1906 a 6-foot diameter well was sunk 234 feet into chalk to supply Flamborough village, the water being pumped to a 50,000 gallon reservoir at 230 feet O.D., and later a 6-foot diameter well, sunk 300 feet deep into chalk at Hunmanby, in 1915, supplied the village from a 60,000 gallon reservoir at 370 feet O.D. Sewerby village was joined to Bridlington's distribution system in 1924 and in 1933 a 24-inch diameter borehole was sunk at the Mill Lane Pumping Station to supply the villages of Marton, Sewerby and Flamborough, as well as the northern part of Bridlington itself. A main link was laid to Flamborough in case of emergency.

Two small private supplies existed at Thorpe Hall, Rudston and at Hunmanby Hall School. The 5-foot diameter, 10 feet deep well at Rudston was constructed in 1903, the water being pumped into a 12,500 gallon reservoir, but the date of construction of the Hunmanby well is unknown.

The Bridlington Corporation Act of 1933 led to the drawing up, in 1934, of a 'regional scheme' to supply 13 parishes in Bridlington Rural District and part of Driffield Rural District with mains water. (Driffield subsequently contracted out of the scheme). The population of Bridlington R.D. in 1934 was 8,160, in an area of 66,903 acres, and the thirteen parishes had only an inadequate supply from surface springs or wells which were often shallow and polluted, e.g. Wilsthorpe Well. The 'regional scheme' involved the construction of a pumping station and two 16-inch diameter boreholes sunk into chalk at Burton Agnes. Mains were laid to villages and part of the Rural District was being supplied by July 1936. The area supplied from Burton Agnes Pumping Station was low-lying land to the west and south-west of Bridlington and also new housing estate development on the south-western outskirts of the town.

III. Rosedale Open Reservoir, Filey, constructed in 18

IV. Scarborough Road Reservoir, Bridlington, constructed in 19

Surplus water from the pumping station was discharged into the town reservoirs at Mill Lane Pumping Station. This latter station was supplying the villages of Bempton, Buckton, Reighton, Grindale, Burton Fleming, Wold Newton, Octon, Thwing, Boynton and Rudston in the north as part of the 'regional scheme'. Reservoirs were constructed in this area in 1937 at Thwing village, Beacon Hill, Speeton, Spell Howe, Hunmanby and Octon village. The smaller reservoir (60,000 gallons) at Hunmanby pumping station was constructed in 1915 and the second (150,000 gallons) in 1936, to provide extra storage when the villages of Muston and Flotmanby were linked to the Hunmanby distribution system in 1937. The second pumping station existing prior to 1934 was Flamborough, which was disused after 1953 because of water pollution in the well.

The 'regional scheme' was completed and formally opened on October 27th, 1938, although affection for the old village well died slowly. Prejudice in the villages over the new mains supply was, however, gradually overcome and farmers in particular benefitted from a piped water supply through improved milk production. During the 1939–1945 war the Rural District mains supply proved of vital importance for service establishments.

After the Second World War the demand for water again increased for farm improvements, increased residential development in Bridlington, and particularly for the increasing number of summer visitors to the resort and to the caravan and chalet sites along the coast. The drought year of 1949 accentuated the urgent need for increased water supplies for peak summer demand was beginning to exceed the safe yield of existing sources. In addition, the Bridlington Corporation Water Order of 1949 transferred the Rural District water undertaking to Bridlington Corporation and extended the Corporation's supply area, by including Folkton and Muston parishes, to cover all 28 villages in an area of 105 square miles.

As part of a development scheme prepared by the Corporation, a 36-inch diameter borehole, 250 feet deep was constructed in chalk at Haisthorpe in 1955, from which the Corporation was authorized to abstract up to 1,500,000 gallons, and mains extensions were carried out at Flixton and Folkton, Flamborough, Hunmanby, Fordon, Burton Agnes, Reighton, Speeton and Buckton to improve the distribution of water.

In 1956 an 18-inch main was laid from the new Haisthorpe borehole to Mill Lane and in 1957 new pumping plant and chlorination equipment were installed in Burton Agnes Pumping Station, a 500,000 gallon reservoir was constructed on Woldgate, the pumping station was completed at Haisthorpe borehole, the new Wold Newton Booster Station and two service reservoirs ensured supplies to Fordon and Thwing, and modern water treatment plant was installed at Mill Lane Pumping Station. Thus by 1958 all 28 villages were receiving piped water supplies, and with the new source at Haisthorpe now operating, the Corporation's water undertaking was in an extremely sound position, with a considerable available margin over peak holiday demand, although further development of the Haisthorpe source is envisaged if the demand for water increases rapidly. Further main extensions from Burton Agnes to Lissett in 1959–1960 improved supplies in the extreme southern portion of the statutory area.

Bridlington Corporation's water undertaking was superseded by the E.Y. (W.A.) W.B. on 1st April, 1962.

Hornsea

Hornsea Local Government Board obtained a loan for the construction of waterworks at Atwick Road, north of the town, and in 1876 a 265-foot borehole was sunk into chalk, followed by a second well and borehole adjacent to the Atwick Road Pumping Station, and reaching a depth of 240 feet. The population had increased from 533 in 1801 to 2,381 by 1901, and the number of inns, hotels and lodging houses had increased from eight in 1831 to 81 in 1901. The Council were thus obliged to sink a third borehole in 1910, in Sissons Field, to increase water supplies. This bore was deepened in 1914 to increase the yield, but was abandoned in 1927 owing to the increasing salinity of the water. A fourth borehole, sunk at Bewholme Lane after 1921, was also abandoned in 1927. The water from all the Hornsea boreholes not only needed treatment to eliminate iron and to neutralize organic impurities, but was also hard and of variable salinity, depending on pumping rate.

Between 1902 and 1922 the population of Hornsea almost doubled, reaching 4,279 in the June 1922 census, and existing water supplies became inadequate to meet summer demand. Silcock (1922) reported unsatisfactory plant at all pumping stations and an inadequate total yield of 89,400 g.p.d. from all bores. He recommended that an exploratory borehole should be sunk into chalk at Aike to obtain 200,000 g.p.d., having discounted alternative schemes to abstract water from Hornsea Mere, due to pollution, and the prohibitive cost of purchasing water from Hull Corporation. However, Hull Corporation successfully objected that Hornsea intended to abstract more water than was required, and that Hull could utilise the water better and so Hornsea was obliged to enter into agreement with Hull Corporation on 11th June, 1926 for the bulk supply of water in perpetuity.

This bulk supply to the Hornsea boundary was inaugurated on May 12th, 1927 and the Hornsea pumping stations were closed down in the same year. As a result, no difficulty has subsequently been found in supplying Hornsea's growing demands, even though the population increased from 4,317 in 1931 to 5,750 in 1961, with the growth of the town's popularity as a seaside resort. From 1st October, 1963 the water undertaking was transferred to Hull Corporation who extended their limits of supply to include Hornsea itself under the provisions of a Kingston upon Hull Water Order of 1963.

Withernsea

The population of the two settlements of Withernsea and Owthorne increased very slowly from 165 persons in 1801 to 272 in 1851. After the railway reached Withernsea in 1854, however, the population increased steadily with the growing popularity of the seaside resort. Between 1861 and 1901 the population grew from 626 to 1,426 and in 1898 Withernsea became an urban district. The number of inns, hotels and lodging houses increased from 37 in 1858 to 53 in 1901, and the town was becoming a service centre for the surrounding rural area. Owthorne was incorporated with Withernsea in 1911, by which time it had become clear that the existing water supplies from shallow wells and storage cisterns were fast becoming totally inadequate. Accordingly, in 1916, an agreement was reached by which Withernsea would purchase from Hull a bulk supply of water to be piped under pressure to Rimswell water tower on the town boundary from where it would be distributed gravitationally by the local water undertaking. Hull Corporation Water Undertaking erected the tower two-and-a-half miles west of Withernsea and laid the main from Hull to Rimswell.

Between 1931 and 1951 the population of Withernsea increased from 4,251 to 5,098, although the 1961 figure showed a decrease to 4,840. The resort was becoming increasingly popular both for day visitors, particularly from Hull, and for campers and caravan holidaymakers. It was estimated, in 1960, that these caravan and chalet sites increased the summer population by between 700 and 800, and in 1961 the town surveyor estimated a summer increase in population from 4,840 to approximately 9,000, with additional increases at week-ends from May to September—rising to 5,000 per day in July and August. From 1st October, 1963, the Water Undertaking (like that of Hornsea) was transferred to the Hull Corporation.

Beverley

The Beverley Waterworks Company was incorporated under the Beverley Waterworks Act, 1881, its works consisting of a well sunk in 1881 at Woodmansey, which was deepened to 320 feet in 1900, and from which a population of 11,425 was initially supplied. Because of steadily increasing demand the Corporation took over the supply in 1907, and by 1922 demand had reached twice the 1881 figure and 550,000 g.p.d. was being pumped from the original well, from a second well sunk to 190 feet in 1900, and from bores sunk in the floor of adit extensions to the second well in 1914. Only by pumping these wells and adits for more than nine hours every day was an adequate supply maintained and in 1921, and other dry years, the water level was so reduced that the pumps drew air.

Several villages in Beverley Rural District had a piped water supply prior to 1933. South Dalton, Holme on the Wolds, and four nearby farms, were supplied privately from the Dalton Holme estate. This supply was obtained from a 90-foot deep chalk well, from which water was pumped into an 80,000 gallon reservoir at 225 feet O.D. The earlier steam-driven pumps were replaced by diesel in 1900 and later by electricity and now pump approximately 427,000 gallons per week. South Cave was supplied from about 1872 by the South Cave Water Company from three springs whose outflow was piped into a reservoir at Spring Head at 180 feet O.D., from which water flowed by gravity through a 2-inch diameter main to South Cave market place. In 1912 the Company was supplying 1,000 people and Fairbank commented on the variable yield of the springs which ranged between 6,000 g.p.d. and 100,000 g.p.d.

Before the 1939–1945 war large parts of Beverley R.D. obtained water from Howden's North Newbald Pumping Station. By means of a booster station and rising main, water was pumped to a 50,000 gallon reservoir on the Wolds at High Hunsley, from where the supply gravitated to parishes on the eastern dip slope of the Wolds. In 1946 this source was supplying 129,000 g.p.d. to Beverley R.D.

In 1942 Beverley R.D.C. purchased the South Cave Water Company, which was in an obsolete condition because of the cumulative effect of inadequate mains, the age and condition of mains and services, the absence of stop taps and the haphazard development of the springs. For several years prior to 1942, supply to the village of South Cave had been restricted during periods of low spring yield and the Water Company had been reluctant to take on additional consumers. In 1942 the water shortage was aggravated by drought and by extra demands for a newly-constructed prisoner-of-war camp and so Beverley R.D.C. obtained permission to take supplementary supplies of water from a private main supplying an Army Camp at Cave Castle from the Howden R.D.C. system at Everthorpe. After 1942 repairs were carried out on the mains, pumps, automatic control gear, and balancing reservoir and automatic chlorination plant was installed.

The demand of 4,470 g.p.d. in 1944 from the population of 298 in Ellerker parish was entirely met from shallow wells and bores, and mains water was necessary before any housing development could take place. Brantingham village was also dependent on shallow wells, though part of the parish was supplied by Elloughton and Brough Water Company. The policy of Beverley R.D.C. was to avoid small, independent pumping stations because of high running expenses and difficulties of supervision. Accordingly, in 1944 they proposed to develop the existing gravitational supply from springs 1 and 2 at South Cave, and to take supplementary supplies from the Howden R.D.C. main at Everthorpe. An additional reservoir (100,000 gallons) was constructed to improve the storage for this south-western part of the Rural District, and mains and services were relaid in South Cave, and installed in Ellerker and Brantingham parishes. The average yield of South Cave Springs 1 and 2 was sufficient to supply an estimated demand, in 1944, of 27,000 g.p.d.

in full for eight months, and an estimated future demand of 50,000 g.p.d. in full for five months of the year.

A co-ordination scheme between the Rural Districts of Beverley, Howden and Pocklington was agreed in 1945 (see p. 37) and in 1949 the 'regional scheme' to extend mains water supply throughout Beverley R.D. started. The demand for water was steadily increasing due to farm improvement schemes, the extension of sewerage schemes in villages, and the increasing population of commuters in all the parishes adjacent to Hull. In estimating future mains water requirements, an agricultural supply of 2·66 gallons per acre was provided. If full treatment sewage disposal schemes were provided, or proposed, for the parish, a domestic supply of 30 g.p.h.p.d. was given, and 20 g.p.h.p.d. in the case of partial treatment sewage disposal schemes.

Beverley R.D.C. had four sources of supply for the increasing mains network provided after 1949. A bulk supply from Driffield R.D.C. served Lund and Lockington parishes in the north. Beverley Corporation supplied water in bulk to the service reservoir at Walkington to supply the parishes of Bishop Burton, Cherry Burton, Walkington and Molescroft to the west of Beverley town, and to part of Woodmansey parish south of Beverley. Hull Corporation served nearby parishes with a direct supply, and the South Cave Springs formed the Rural District's only source of its own, supplying the south-western parishes and supplemented by water from the North Newbald Pumping Station.

Agreement was reached in 1948 between the Beverley and Hull Corporations for a bulk supply from the latter to be delivered at the Woodmansey Reservoir for distribution by Beverley Corporation. This was necessitated by pollution in boreholes and by the variable yield of existing supplies. At the end of 1950, 4,350 houses in Beverley R.D. (79·38%) had mains water and by 1960 the number was 6,407. The number of houses dependent on private wells and springs decreased between 1950 and 1960 from 1,120 (20·62%) to 589 (8·42%), but 326 private wells and 171 communal wells were still in existence at the end of the period. The water supply position at the end of 1960 is summarized in Table 7.

On 1st April, 1962, the parishes of the Beverley R.D. not included in the statutory area of supply of the Hull Corporation, were taken over by the E.Y. (W.A.) W.B. and from 1st October, 1963, the

TABLE 7

Parish	Number of Houses	Mains Supplies			Bores and Wells			Other		
		Own Tap	Common Stand-pipe	Street Stand-pipe	Own Well	Common Well	Street Well	Springs	Rain-water	No Water
eswick	98	68	—	—	18	—	—	7	—	5
ishop Burton	128	118	6	—	2	—	—	—	2	—
rantingham	121	113	4	—	2	—	—	—	1	1
ave, South	509	476	3	—	10	7	—	3	2	8
herry Burton	123	105	5	—	8	3	—	—	—	2
alton Holme	96	78	9	—	2	—	—	—	2	5
llerker	105	95	2	—	5	—	—	—	2	1
lloughton	995	977	—	4	7	5	—	—	—	2
tton	114	89	—	—	—	25	—	—	—	—
erriby, North	823	812	11	—	—	—	—	—	—	—
econfield	121	83	—	—	24	10	—	4	—	—
even	264	170	8	—	33	39	—	2	—	12
ockington	160	136	—	—	12	8	—	2	—	2
und	106	89	12	—	3	—	—	—	2	—
Iolescroft	468	453	—	—	12	3	—	—	—	—
Iewbald	210	198	4	—	5	—	—	—	1	2
outh	36	25	—	—	9	2	—	—	—	—
owley	228	184	5	9	10	3	3	—	10	4
kidby	255	234	9	—	3	7	—	—	—	2
wanland	490	480	10	—	—	—	—	—	—	—
ickton	183	109	5	—	38	31	—	—	—	—
Valkington	265	242	3	19	—	—	—	—	—	1
Vawne	175	124	18	4	15	12	—	1	1	1
Velton	416	361	3	42	1	8	—	—	—	—
Voodmansey	507	388	5	—	107	5	—	—	—	2
Total	6,996	6,207	122	78	326	168	3	19	23	50

HOUSE WATER SUPPLIES, BEVERLEY R.D.C., 1960

Source:— Annual Report of the Medical Officer of Health for Beverley R.D.C.

Beverley Corporation's water undertaking was transferred to the Hull Corporation, by the terms of the Order previously referred to in connection with Hornsea and Withernsea.

Driffield

Incorporated under the Driffield and District Water Act of 1882, the Driffield Water Company supplied the parishes and town of Great Driffield, Little Driffield and Nafferton, i.e. an area of approximately five square miles ranging in height between 50 and 100 feet O.D.

Spellowgate Pumping Station, which was constructed about one-and-a-half miles north of Driffield in 1883, contained a 157-foot well in the Middle Chalk extended by a further 30 feet of 18-inch diameter borehole. Gas engines and pumps were installed in 1885 to deliver 15,000 g.p.h. to an adjacent covered reservoir (397,000 gallons) which was constructed in 1884 and from which water gravitated to Driffield. This pumping station is still in use although electric pumps were installed in 1950. The Local Government Board sank a borehole at North End Driffield in about 1890, for a private owner who subsequently sold it to the Water Company in 1912. This was used as a stand-by source, the pumps being capable of delivering 11,000 g.p.h. directly into the mains.

In 1930 a population of 3,552 in 863 houses was supplied by the Water Company and 2,122 people in 510 houses were still supplied from 334 private pumps in Driffield. Even in 1945, many houses in Driffield still used a pump for water supply and even some houses with mains water, retained an outside pump to be used in the garden or as an emergency supply. A population of 4,000 was supplied in 1945, with approximately 1,672 still using private bores.

The Driffield Water Order of 1948 gave powers to continue and maintain North End Pumping Station, to construct an additional borehole at this station, and to raise additional capital up to £8,000. The need for this additional borehole arose from increased demands for water consequent upon an influx of population into Driffield after the war, and from the condemning of supplies from several private pumps. In addition, water levels in the chalk fell from 1942 to 1943 and again in June 1944. Of the 4,000 consumers in 1945, some had no W.C. and an additional 2,200 would want a mains supply if the water carriage system were adopted. The resulting

V. Nafferton Pumping Station, built in 19

VI. Spaldington Water Tower, built in 19

increase in consumption for 3,960 people at 25 g.p.h.p.d., would mean an increased daily domestic demand of 100,000 g.p.d. above the 1945 consumption of 133,000 g.p.d.

A new pump, installed in 1950 in the North End borehole, was by 1961 being operated for 9 hours per day, pumping 17,500 g.p.h. direct to supply only during periods of peak demand, any surplus water being pumped up to the Spellowgate Reservoir. Even in the dry summer of 1959, the minimum water level in the North End borehole during pumping was three feet from the top of the bore. (The water level recovers quickly on cessation of pumping at this source). The Spellowgate well and borehole remained the main source until 1962, when the Driffield Water Company was taken over by the E.Y. (W.A.) W.B. on 1st April. Three private boreholes in Driffield were still in use (by Glaxo Laboratories Limited, Driffield Laundry and Taylors Ironmongers) in 1960.

Turning now to Driffield Rural District, a scheme was proposed by Fairbank in 1908 to supply the village of Nafferton with a piped water supply. The Local Government Board provided a partial loan and specified the provision, if practicable, of a public water supply of not less than 15 g.p.h.p.d. The Nafferton works were, in fact, designed to supply a population of 1,200 at 20 g.p.h.p.d. A 6-foot diameter well, 216 feet deep, was sunk into chalk with a further 50-foot borehole in the bottom of the well. The well and borehole were completed, in 1910, on Nafferton Wold (262 feet O.D.), about two miles north of Nafferton Station. The pumping station contained the well pumps and an oil engine, whilst a wind engine was mounted on a 40-foot high steel tower. A concrete storage reservoir was constructed adjacent to the pumping station (Plate V) and the Nafferton works were opened on 21st May, 1912.

In 1915, 1,000 people in 200 houses, five farms and two schools were supplied in Nafferton and by 1924, additional demands were being satisfied from eleven farms (for stock and threshing), five cow keepers, 21 baths, one milk cooling apparatus, 45 water closets, one motor sewage pump, one water motor for a Wesleyan organ and five public houses. This increase in consumption in g.p.h.p.d. is shown in Table 8. Water meters were installed in Nafferton in 1926 in an attempt to eliminate a wastage equivalent to 18 g.p.h.p.d.

A pumping station was constructed at Hutton Cranswick in 1940, consisting of two 15-inch diameter boreholes sunk to a depth

TABLE 8

Year	Average Consumption by 1,000 people in g.p.h.p.d.
1915	7·46
1916	8·73
1919	10·70
1922	16·80
1923	17·60
1924	20·21

AVERAGE CONSUMPTION IN NAFFERTON, 1915-24

of 86 feet in chalk. In 1949 the Rural District water supply was provided by this source and by the Nafferton Pumping Station. The maximum capacity of the pumps at Nafferton was 7,000 g.p.h., and 15,500 g.p.h. at Hutton Cranswick, and this supply was equally fed by boosters into the high level western and low level eastern areas. The scheme was designed to provide for a total demand for all purposes of 30 g.p.h.p.d. The Hutton Cranswick booster pumped water to Summit Reservoir at 490 ft. O.D., while the Garton booster supplied Sledmere, Langtoft and adjacent northern Wolds parishes from Collingwood Reservoir at 585 ft. O.D. Wetwang Booster, drawing water from Summit reservoir, supplied the highest north-western parishes of Fimber and Fridaythorpe from Towthorpe Reservoir, and Nafferton Pumping Station supplied the low-lying eastern area.

Plate V shows Nafferton Pumping Station at the edge of a chalk pit, with the possibility of pollution of the supply. Moore (1949) suggested the construction of a new pumping station at Kilham to replace the Nafferton source, which would then revert to an emergency stand-by station. In 1950 a new borehole of 15 inches diameter and 355 feet depth was sunk into chalk outside the Hutton Cranswick Pumping Station and yielded a minimum of 10,000 g.p.h. Kilham Pumping Station consisted of two 15-inch diameter chalk boreholes, 200 and 100 feet deep respectively, pumping and chlorination equipment and an adjacent covered reservoir. The boreholes were first pumped on 14 February, 1958 and were tested in 1959 at 70,000 g.p.h., with little consequent fall in water level; a reliable yield of 1,000,000 g.p.d. was subsequently achieved. This station started to supply the northern and north-eastern part of the Rural District after 1960, when ten farms were connected to new mains and eventually the Nafferton Station was used only as a standby source; Kilham water, by then, supplied the lower eastern part, the water being boosted to Nafferton Reservoir and supplied by gravity from there.

In addition to the ten farms supplied from the Kilham boreholes after 1960, via the 300,000 gallon Maiden's Grave Reservoir at 360 feet O.D., which was constructed in 1956, the Kilham Booster also supplied this reservoir with water for Garton village. The 2,000 g.p.h. booster at Garton then pumped the surplus water to Collingwood Reservoir (capacity 100,000 gallons). Metered supplies were given to six farms in Norton R.D. and bulk supplies to Bridlington Corporation at Octon cross-roads and to Beverley R.D., until 1962, in order to supply the parish of Lund.

Of an estimated population of 10,730 in mid-1959, about 980 were without piped supplies. These included 300 houses, isolated high Wolds farms, individual houses in Beeford, North Frodingham and lower areas, and about 50 people in Nafferton village who still relied on springs for water supply.

The Driffield R.D.C. Water Undertaking was superseded by the E.Y. (W.A.) W.B. on 1st April, 1962 and it is probable that the distribution system will be modified.

Norton

Norton's original water supply was through a main laid across the River Derwent from Malton when Norton was included in Malton Borough. The town became an Urban District in about 1894. In 1892 an 8-foot diameter well was sunk 25 feet into Lower Oolite Limestone at Howe Hill and from the bottom of this, two boreholes of 12-inch and 9-inch diameter were sunk a further 52 feet. A 250,000 gallons reservoir had been constructed nearby, in 1891, at 170 feet O.D. Pumps installed in 1893 delivered 14,000 g.p.h. into the reservoir, from whence the water gravitated to mains in Norton.

The population increased from 3,842 in 1901 to 3,935 in 1931, and in 1934 Fairbank, estimating the water requirements of Malton and Norton at 280,000 g.p.d., proposed new borehole pumps to provide this quantity at Howe Hill Pumping Station. By 1937 the demand for both towns was 330,000 g.p.d. and between 1936 and 1952, a bulk supply was pumped directly to Malton and to Malton's reservoir, as an emergency measure. In 1954 the pumps at Howe Hill were modernized and a mains extension scheme, to increase water pressure in the town, was carried out.

In Norton Rural District each village had its own spring supply prior to 1933 (see Table 9) although a 'regional scheme' was prepared to supply mains water from four spring sources after 1934. The Acklam Spring was first used in 1936, although reservoirs

TABLE 9

Location of Spring	Approximate Yield of Spring (g.p.d.)	Area Supplied
Birdsall (chalk)	Not known	Birdsall Hall and village, North Grimston Hall and village, and 4 or 5 farms
Burythorpe (Jurassic limestone)	13,000	Burythorpe village and parish (part)
East Heslerton (chalk)	20,000	East Heslerton village and parish (part)
Rillington (gravel)	9,915	Rillington village and parish (part)
Leavening (not known)	Not known	Leavening village and parish (part)
Scagglethorpe (chalk)	6,000	Scagglethorpe village and parish (part)
Settrington (gravel)	7,425	Settrington village and parish (part)
Thorpe Bassett (chalk)	11,520	Thorpe Bassett village (part)
Wintringham (chalk)	Not known	Wintringham village and parish (part)
Yedingham (artesian well)	1,755	Yedingham village and parish (part)

VILLAGE SPRING SUPPLIES IN NORTON R.D. BEFORE 1933

were not constructed at Acklam until 1952. Mains were laid from this source to supply the villages of Leppington, Scrayingham, Westow, Langton, Kennythorpe, Burythorpe and Menethorpe in the west. The Stackhills Spring was first used in 1936, water being pumped up to 350 feet O.D., from where it gravitated to the villages of Wintringham, Rillington and Thorpe Bassett in the north-west and to Knapton whilst a second set of pumps delivered water to Settrington Beacon to supply high Wolds farms. The Sherburn Spring supplied villages in the northern part of the Rural District, and was also linked to the Stackhills Spring mains to the west, and to Sherburn, Ganton and Willerby to the east. Water was pumped from this source to the south-western high Wolds area and to Binnington Wold high farms.

Water from the Wharram Percy Spring was pumped to a service reservoir at Wharram Le Street, at 560 feet O.D., from which gravity mains supplied the parishes of Wharram, Kirby Grindalythe, Luttons, Weaverthorpe and Foxholes in the Great Wold Valley. A small independent supply was also pumped from the Wharram Percy Spring to a 5,000 gallon tank at 680 feet O.D., in order to supply four farms lying above the service reservoir level. The Wharram Spring was supplying 25,000 g.p.d. in 1937.

Pocklington R.D.C. agreed in 1953 to deliver water in bulk to two points on the Norton R.D. boundary at Thixendale in the Wolds, from where Norton R.D.C. would distribute it in their mains. A similar connection was made in 1959 between the Norton U.D.C. mains and those of Norton R.D.C. at the town boundary on Langton Road, thereby ensuring an automatic emergency supply of 20,000 g.p.d. to the Acklam Regional (western area) Scheme if mains pressure fell below a specified figure. Driffield R.D.C. agreed to supply six farms in Norton R.D. (see p. 29).

Associated British Maltsters Limited opened a silo at Knapton in 1954 and Norton R.D.C. agreed to supply water at a maximum rate of 20,000 g.p.d. A booster plant was installed at the Stackhills Spring to provide sufficient head for the additional flow to the silo. As this firm expanded, consumption increased rapidly, trebling between 1954 and 1958, so that in May 1959 another booster was installed at Heslerton. With a further request for additional water in 1960, a mains connection was constructed across the River Derwent between Yedingham, in Norton R.D., and Marishes in the statutory area of the Ryedale Joint Water Board (R. J.W.B.). This supply was started in June 1961.

In October 1957 Norton R.D.C. took over the Leavening parish spring supply, which had been inaugurated in 1913 and which consisted of a spring, collecting tank, and mains and in November

1959 water from the Stackhills Spring filled the Washdyke Reservoir above Thorpe Bassett village, part of which had formerly been supplied by a private supply.

The Wharram Percy source suffered the disadvantages of difficulty of access, liability to pollution, the necessity for continuous chlorination and a variable yield which often proved unreliable in drought periods. On 29th December, 1959, for example, after a very dry year, the output was 60 g.p.m. and because of difficulties in maintaining the supply, an emergency supply of 6,000 gallons per night was received from Driffield R.D.C. The average daily consumption from the Wharram source in 1959 was 55 g.p.h., and the booster installed at Wharram Le Street operated continuously to maintain the supply. Consequently, the Wold Valley Scheme was started, whereby the surplus yield of the Sherburn Spring would be pumped to a 100,000 gallon reservoir at 517 feet O.D. on Sherburn Wold and would then gravitate to Weaverthorpe through a 6-inch diameter main and be pumped up the Great Wold Valley to Wharram Percy through a 4-inch diameter main. From August 1960, the Sherburn source supplied the Wold Valley and after April 1961, the Wharram source supplied only the high Wolds farms. The Wold Valley scheme was finally completed in 1962.

The Norton R.D.C. water undertaking was superseded by the R.J.W.B. on 1st October, 1961.

Market Weighton

Incorporated under the Market Weighton Water Order, 1884, and amended by the Water Undertaking (Modification of Charges) Act of 1921, the Market Weighton Water Company supplied an area within a one mile radius from the green in Market Weighton, together with the village of Goodmanham. The pumping station was constructed in 1885 at Goodmanham, and contained a 6-foot diameter well, 40 feet deep into chalk, with a 12-inch diameter borehole sunk a further 40 feet below the well bottom, and duplicate steam-driven pumps, which were replaced in 1932 by two oil-driven pumps. Water is pumped from the well, through a rising main, to a 150,000 gallon service reservoir above the pumping station, from whence it gravitates to Market Weighton.

A number of mains extensions were carried out after 1934 and the Water Company was purchased on 1st January, 1955 by

Pocklington R.D.C., and since 1st April, 1962 has been included in the statutory area of the E.Y. (W.A.) W.B.

Pocklington

Works were constructed by the Pocklington Water Company Limited under Provisional Orders dated 1889, 1893 and 1935, to supply that part of the parish of Pocklington which lay within a distance of half-a-mile from the north corner of the church, excepting the portion within the parish of Barmby Moor.

The source of supply was the Whitekeld Beck springs north of Pocklington, the first spring being collected in a covered chamber in 1893. The original main, laid in 1893, was extended in 1910 and 1915, when waters from a second and third spring were collected. This main conveyed water to a pumphouse from which it was delivered to a 150,000 gallon reservoir, constructed in 1893 on Chapel Hill (190 feet O.D.), and then flowed by gravity to Pocklington's mains, most of which were laid in 1889. In 1935 a new main was laid from the pumphouse on the west side of Whitekeld Beck, to collect water from a fourth spring which was then pumped to the reservoir. The Water Company's supply could be augmented in times of shortage, at Pocklington parish boundary, where a connection existed with the Pocklington R.D.C. main.

Attempts were made in 1955 to augment the Water Company's supplies when Fairbank located and gauged 18 springs but only four of these were sufficiently reliable to warrant collection. Fairbank deduced that the minimum total available spring water resources in White Keld Valley would not exceed 156,000 g.p.d., which would give only a meagre excess over an anticipated future demand of 150,000 g.p.d. In 1955 the flow was, in fact, limited by mains capacity to 120,000 g.p.d. and the Company regularly took a supply from the Rural District in times of shortage in 1955 and 1956. Due to numerous complaints of inadequate supply from residents in Pocklington, the Water Company was finally purchased by Pocklington R.D.C. on 1st October, 1957, and has been included in the statutory area of the E.Y. (W.A.) W.B. since 1st April, 1962.

Turning now to Pocklington Rural District itself, nine parishes had a piped water supply to a total population of 3,812 prior to 1933. At Barmby upon the Moor a population of 548 was supplied from a 280-foot deep borehole sunk in 1907 in Red Shale. A windmill lifted water to a 40,000 gallon elevated water tank, from which it flowed by gravity to service mains in the village. In 1933 the estimated consumption was 6,000 g.p.d. A population of 55 in Great Givendale with Grimthorpe received a standpipe supply from a spring, piped as part of a private supply for a Mr. Ford, whilst another standpipe supply, to 282 people in Kirby Underdale with Garrowby, was obtained from the private spring supply of Lord Halifax.

Most of the population of 304 in Londesborough with Easthorpe were supplied by service mains from a spring at 300 feet O.D. piped by J. Lupton Booth. As previously discussed, the Market Weighton Water Company supplied 1,994 people in Market Weighton, Arras and Goodmanham and the population of 13 in the parish of Ousethorpe was supplied by Pocklington Water Company. A bore-hole sunk in 1909 in Keuper Marl supplied 411 people in Shipton-thorpe, a windmill pump lifting water into a 20,000 gallon elevated tank, from whence it flowed by gravity at a rate of 4,500 g.p.d. in 1915. The ninth piped supply was by standpipe at Thixendale, where 205 villagers relied on a spring which supplied 3,000 g.p.d. in 1915.

The parishes of Millington with Little Givendale and Sancton with Houghton, with 139 and 356 people respectively, were supplied by springs with no service pipes, whilst Fridaythorpe and Huggate parishes on the Wolds, with 233 and 382 people respectively, relied entirely on rain water, and the remaining 33 parishes, containing 5,709 people, obtained supplies from shallow wells. All these parishes were situated in the Vale of York.

A 'regional scheme' was prepared by Haiste for Pocklington R.D.C. in 1934 in which he assumed 10 g.p.h.p.d. for existing requirements and 20 g.p.h.p.d. for future requirements. He measured spring flows at Kirby Underdale, Bishop Wilton, Great Givendale, Millington, Warter, Sancton and North Newbald, and as a result of his report work started on the 'regional scheme' in 1934 with the development of the Warter and Millington Springs, the laying of trunk and distribution mains in the central and southern zones, and the construction of reservoirs at Millington, Warter, Bishop Wilton, Garrowby and Sancton.

Howden R.D.C. were given a bulk supply at Ellerton and Harswell on the R.D. boundary in 1935 and in 1939 and 1940,

Pocklington R.D.C. sealed the Kirby Underdale Springs, laid mains from these to link with the existing system at Bugthorpe, and duplicated mains supplying new Air Ministry Establishments. In 1945 all these works were purchased by the Council, and in the same year a Co-ordination Scheme was agreed (see p. 37).

As a result of increasing demand for water two 100,000 gallon reservoirs were constructed at Garrowby and Waterman Hole in 1947, in addition to a pumping station at Kirby Underdale and a balancing tank at Millington Pumping Station. In 1950 a reservoir was constructed at Loaningdale and 25 mains extensions were installed to serve local high level farms on the Wolds, and the Council also took over the Londesborough village supply (see p. 34) in the same year. Givendale Reservoir was constructed in 1952 and Loaningdale, Burnby and Londesborough reservoirs in 1954.

Haiste designed the 'regional scheme' so that the Rural District would be supplied with water in a northern, central and southern zone, and so that surplus water could be supplied to any zone through a system of interconnected mains. By 1960, bulk supplies were given to Howden R.D.C. at four points and to Norton R.D.C. at Thixendale and Hanging Grimston Wold, and sealed main connections, which could be used in times of emergency, existed at Elvington on the Derwent R.D. boundary and Stamford Bridge on the Flaxton R.D. boundary.

The Council purchased the Market Weighton Water Company on 1st January, 1955 (see p. 32) and the Pocklington Water Company on 1st October, 1957 (see p. 33).

Haiste (1959) reported in August, 1959 that consumption in the Rural Districts of Beverley, Howden and Pocklington had reached the figure estimated in 1956, and that the distribution system was unable to deal with the increased consumption. He repeated his suggestion of 1956 that the Market Weighton borehole be developed and connected to Bishop Burton in Beverley R.D., thereby allowing the northern area of Beverley R.D. to be supplied from the Market Weighton source and reducing demands by Beverley R.D.C. on the Howden R.D.C. source at North Newbald Pumping Station. As a result of a Ministry Inquiry into water supply schemes for the Rural Districts of Beverley, Howden, and Pocklington held in January 1959, Pocklington R.D.C. sealed the Londesborough Springs and laid a main from the springs to Market Weighton. At the end of

1959 the Market Weighton borehole was test pumped over 14 days and a minimum yield of 365,000 g.p.d. was obtained, of which Haiste proposed to make 250,000 g.p.d. available to Beverley R.D.C. and 150,000 g.p.d. to Pocklington R.D.C. for the Market Weighton and Goodmanham areas, and to Howden R.D.C. for the Sancton and Cliff areas.

By January 1962 a 6-inch diameter main had been laid from the Market Weighton Pumping Station into Cherry Burton and repairs had been carried out at the pumping station. Mains were being laid to high farms in Beverley R.D. to connect with the trunk main and the construction of a reservoir at Arras was proposed. The water from the pumping station reservoir was to be boosted through the 6-inch main to the Arras Reservoir and from thence gravitated to Bishop Burton.

In 1962 Pocklington R.D.C. supplied a mainly agricultural area with only a small demand by light industry in Pocklington, Market Weighton and Stamford Bridge. The water undertaking was superseded by the E.Y. (W.A.) W.B. on 1st April, 1962.

Howden

The market town of Howden received a water supply from the Asselby Pumping Station which was constructed in 1889. Water was pumped from a 250-foot well and borehole into adjacent wooden storage tanks of 5,500 gallon capacity and thence to Howden. Mainly because this water had a high turbidity, and contained a large quantity of solids, chlorine and iron, the supply was not developed to serve the Rural District or the expanding town of Howden. The demand for water increased at the beginning of the twentieth century as many of the shallow wells, streams, ponds and water cisterns became polluted and were condemned. Although the population in Howden R.D. actually decreased steadily from 15,001 in 1861 to 12,636 in 1911, the Council were, nevertheless, looking for additional water supplies before 1911 and investigated scarp foot springs at Drewton Manor and North Newbald. Fairbank (1923) was consulted on a water supply for Howden and in 1932 it was proposed to supply 25,000 g.p.d. from Goole, across the River Ouse at Boothferry bridge, the appropriate main being laid in June 1935.

Arising from a specific complaint in 1935, the Local Government Board insisted on the preparation of a scheme to supply the whole Rural District consisting of about 150 square miles of flat, marshy country. In 1937 four bores were sunk to red chalk at North Newbald, a pumping station and reservoir were constructed, and mains supplied water to the parishes of North Cave, Broomfleet, Newport, Gilberdyke, Blacktoft, Laxton and Wressle. Also in 1937, a supply of water was obtained from Pocklington R.D.C. mains at Harswell and East Cottingwith on the Howden R.D. boundary to supply the parishes of Holme-on-Spalding-Moor, Ellerton, Bubwith, Foggathorpe and Spaldington. A collecting tank and booster pumping station were constructed at Harswell and a service reservoir at Holme-on-Spalding-Moor, and mains were laid in these parishes. Thus, by 1939 the 'regional scheme' to supply mains water in Howden R.D. was completed.

In 1945 the Rural Districts of Pocklington, Howden and Beverley agreed on the principle of co-ordinated water supplies proposed by Haiste (1945) in order to fully utilize the surplus spring water available in Pocklington R.D., and the potential yield of North Newbald Pumping Station, and to minimise demands for water on the Borough of Beverley and Driffield R.D.C. (for Beverley R.D.) and on Goole (for Howden R.D.). The improvements, with co-ordination in both Howden and Pocklington, were to increase storage capacity, to increase the capacity of the mains distribution

TABLE 10

Source	Amount g.p.d.
From N. Newbald	267,000
„ Goole	54,000
„ Pocklington R.D.	44,000
Total	365,000
Less supplies to Beverley R.D.C. at South Cave and Newbald from North Newbald Pumping Station	24,000
Net Total	341,000

WATER CONSUMPTION IN HOWDEN R.D., 1948-49

systems, especially near Howden, and to provide supplies sufficient for all future requirements of the two Rural Districts.

The average consumption by the population of 11,730 for the year ending 31st March, 1949 in Howden R.D. is shown in Table 10.

As part of the co-ordination scheme, Howden R.D.C. laid an 8-inch diameter main from Holme-on-Spalding-Moor to Spaldington, where a 100,000 gallon water tower was constructed in 1954 (see Plate VI). During the war years, with service development at Breighton and Holme-on-Spalding-Moor, the North Newbald source was developed by the construction of new bores, and in 1948 further bores were sunk and a 500,000 gallon reservoir was constructed. A further bore sunk at North Newbald in 1954, to meet increasing demands for water, made a total of nine boreholes at this station, all in red chalk and only seven of which were in use. In 1956 the reliable yield of these bores was 450,000 g.p.d., the average consumption was 470,000 g.p.d. and the population supplied was 11,728. By 1961, 98% of Howden R.D. had access to mains water.

The distribution system in Howden R.D. is divided into three zones, the northern zone being supplied in bulk from Pocklington R.D.C. at Laytham, Shipton, Cottingwith and Harswell, the eastern zone from the North Newbald source, and the south-western zone, including Howden, receiving a bulk supply from Goole. Distribution is controlled through valves to equalize the demand in each zone with the fluctuation in the yield from the bores at North Newbald. On 1st April, 1962 the water undertaking was superseded by the E.Y. (W.A.) W.B.

Elloughton and Brough

In May 1887 a report was made by Fairbank on a scheme to provide Elloughton and Brough with a piped water supply, with a subsequent alternative scheme suggested in May 1889. Not until 1906, however, was a committee appointed to investigate and report on the practicability of forming a Waterworks Company. The Brough Water Order of 1908 promoted the Elloughton and Brough Water Company and headworks were designed to supply up to 20 g.p.h.p.d.

Chalk springs in Elloughton Dale, about half-a-mile north-east of Elloughton village, were piped in 1909 to a 60,000 gallon concrete reservoir at 130 feet O.D. In 1914, which was a dry year, the total

VII. Bower's Plan of the Town and Harbour of Kingston upon Hull, 17
Photography by permission of Kingston upon Hull Corporation Water Departme

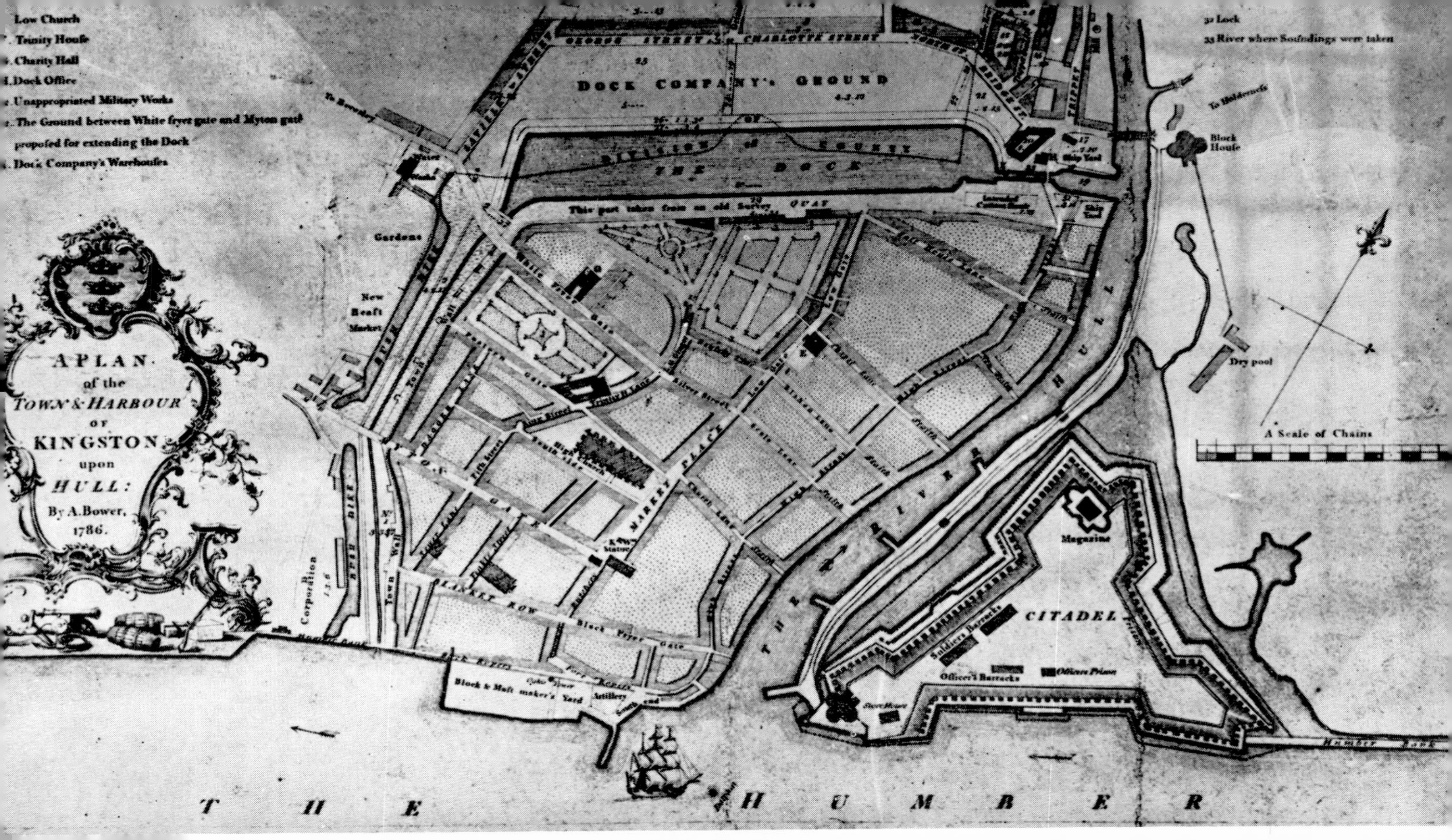
A PLAN of the TOWN & HARBOUR OF KINGSTON upon HULL: By A. Bower, 1786.
Low Church
Trinity House
Charity Hall
Dock Office
Unappropriated Military Works
The Ground between White fryer gate and Myton gate propofed for extending the Dock
Dock Company's Warehoufes
32 Lock
33 River where Soundings were taken
DOCK COMPANY's GROUND
GEORGE STREET
CHARLOTTE STREET
THE DOCK
This part taken from an old Survey
QUAY
To Beverley
To Holderness
Block House
Dry pool
A Scale of Chains
Gardens
New Beast Market
White Fryer Gate
MARKET PLACE
Black Fryer Gate
BLANKET ROW
Church Lane
Ship Yard
Magazine
CITADEL
Soldiers Barracks
Officer's Barracks
Officers Prison
Block & Mast maker's Yard
Artillery
Corporation
THE RIVER HULL
THE HUMBER

flow from these springs was 18,720 g.p.d., and in 1915 the average consumption for 725 consumers was 11,812 g.p.d., which was 16·3 g.p.h.p.d. for domestic and trade consumption. Fairbank reported an abundant yield of water from both springs in 1916, but in October 1917 the Blackburn Aeroplane and Motor Company requested 300 g.p.d. and 16 cottages at Brough requested 1,200 g.p.d., all of which was supplied in 1918. In April 1918 the Water Company supplied 820 consumers with 14·9 g.p.h.p.d. but by 1921, 875 consumers used 19,147 g.p.d., i.e. 21·8 g.p.h.p.d., and a shortage of water resulted. In 1930 Fairbank considered the reliable yield of the Elloughton Dale springs in dry periods was 20,000 g.p.d., and suggested that an additional 40,000 g.p.d. could be obtained from Welton springs as an emergency supply. He reported in February, 1938 on the situation whereby the Company was buying water from Hull Corporation when there was an ample supply from the Elloughton Dale Springs. The Company, in trying to satisfy complaints from consumers, of insufficient pressure in higher properties, had effected a connection with the Hull Corporation's mains to augment the spring supply only when it was insufficient to supply consumers and when the reservoir level had fallen. The main problem was lack of carrying capacity in the mains, in relation to the increased consumption by Blackburn Aircraft Limited and in 1939 this firm reported a sadly deficient supply. The yield of the Elloughton Dale Springs varied from over 100,000 g.p.d. to a minimum of less than 30,000 g.p.d.

Fairbank recorded a domestic consumption in 1938 of 65,000 g.p.d., and a consumption at Blackburns of 48,000 g.p.d. In 1939 the Company was supplying 570 houses with a daily demand of 112 g.p. house. The proposal made by Fairbank in 1940 that Blackburn's should obtain their water direct from Hull Corporation's mains was not carried out, so that in 1950 the firm still suffered a water shortage. Eventually, the situation was reached when the Water Company was principally a water distributing and rate collecting agency for Hull Corporation, and in some years, e.g. 1947, the amount of charges paid to the Corporation exceeded the amount received by the Company in rates.

The Elloughton and Brough Water Company was transferred to the Hull Corporation Water Undertaking in 1956/57. No water was purchased from Hull Corporation after 1956, the Company's statutory area thereafter being supplied as an extension of the Corporation's western supply zone.

Hedon

At the beginning of the twentieth century householders had private wells in Hedon, but as in Howden Rural District, previously mentioned, many of these were becoming polluted and were condemned. This situation led to the Holderness Water Act of 1908 which incorporated the Holderness Water Company to supply Hedon Borough, Hornsea and Withernsea, the Rural Districts of Patrington and Skirlaugh and parts of the Rural Districts of Beverley, Sculcoates and Driffield. However, there seems to be no evidence that this Company ever functioned and in 1914 a bulk supply of water was provided by Hull Corporation at the Hedon Borough boundary, from where the Borough distributed it, and this supply was maintained until 1st October, 1963 when the Borough's water undertaking was transferred to Hull Corporation.

Derwent Rural District

Prior to 1936, water supplies in Derwent R.D. were similar to those in Howden and Pocklington and consisted of marl ponds, shallow wells and roof water collected in cisterns and water butts. In 1936 a regional scheme was designed to supply mains water by gravitation to all parishes in the northern part of the Rural District. The parishes of Water Fulford and Heslington were within the statutory area of York Waterworks Company and were already supplied with mains water in 1936. Thus, the remaining parishes of Dunnington, Kexby, Elvington, Wheldrake, Thorganby with West Cottingwith, Skipwith, North Duffield, Deighton, Escrick and Naburn were to be supplied in the regional scheme. The Council purchased water in bulk from York Waterworks Company which was metered at three points on the boundary, at Hull Road, Selby Road and Naburn Lane.

In the south only the parishes of Barlby and Riccall were supplied with mains water from Selby Water Undertaking. Selby's supply was obtained from two 400-foot bores in Old Red Sandstone, at Brayton Barff. The supply to Derwent R.D. was pumped across the River Ouse to a meter from whence it was distributed by the Rural District undertaking. As storage was non-existent in Derwent R.D.

in 1938, the proper maintenance of these bulk supplies and mains was essential. Barlby parish formed the only industrialized area in the Rural District and a seed-crushing mill, sugar-beet factory, flour mill, tar, distillery and sauce works used large quantities of Selby's water. In 1938 mains extensions were commenced in the remaining parishes in the south i.e. Cliffe, Escrick (part), Hemingbrough, Kelfield and Stillingfleet, using the Selby bulk supply.

The regional scheme for the northern part of the Rural District was designed for a population of 3,904 in 1936, with an estimated maximum demand of 90,300 g.p.d. In 1938 the daily demand for a population of 2,921 in Barlby parish and 739 in Riccall parish was 96,700 gallons, and the population to be supplied in the regional scheme for the other five southern parishes was 2,050.

After the passing of the Rural Water Supplies and Sewerage Act in 1944, Derwent R.D.C. sought to extend a mains supply to almost all of the 100 farms still without a piped water supply, and to a few isolated houses in 1946. Fairbank suggested increasing the supply to the southern area from Selby Waterworks to 300,000 g.p.d., with a duplication of the trunk main across the River Ouse to reduce pressure losses and he estimated an ultimate requirement from the York Waterworks Company of 120,000 g.p.d. for the proposed mains extensions to the northern area. The water towers constructed in 1938 at Dunnington and Wheldrake provided storage of only 60,000 gallons and he proposed to increase storage by means of a 180,000 gallon reservoir at Stillingfleet, which was finally constructed in 1952.

Demand for water from Service establishments, particularly Elvington Aerodrome, increased during the 1939-45 war. Pocklington R.D.C. supplied this aerodrome by a mains connection at Sutton Bridge (see p. 35) and in 1953 the York Waterworks Company laid an 8-inch diameter main from their statutory boundary, but when the aerodrome was closed Derwent R.D.C. used this main to improve their distribution network. Mains extensions to isolated properties were carried out in 1952. A new main from Barlby to augment the supply to Cliffe and Hemingbrough was laid in 1960, and a 100,000 gallon water tower was constructed at Hemingbrough in 1961 to provide the first storage in this southern area. Most of the Barlby industries, mentioned earlier, supplemented mains supplies from their own boreholes.

On 1st April, 1962 the Derwent R.D.C. Water Undertaking in the parishes of Barlby, Cliffe, Hemingbrough, Kelfield and Riccall was transferred to the Pontefract, Goole and Selby Water Board and on 1st April, 1963 the Water Undertaking in the parishes of Dunnington, Kexby, Elvington, Wheldrake, Thorganby, Skipworth, North Duffield, Naburn, Escrick, Deighton and Stillingfleet was transferred to the York Waterworks Company.

Kingston upon Hull

Hull is not mentioned in the Domesday Book, but by the second part of the thirteenth century a settlement known as Wyke had grown up on the eastern side of the River Hull, on the silt and warp foreshore once overrun by tidal waters from the River Humber. In 1293 it was reported (Jones, 1955) that ". . . the town of Wyke is abundantly supplied with fresh water which comes from a place which is called Springhead, some five miles distant from the town". This spring supply flowed to Wyke along a natural stream channel, following the line of the present Spring Bank and Prospect Street, and falling near the eastern end of Waterhouse Lane into a now long extinct outlet of the River Hull.

The town grew, and in 1376, when daily fresh water was being brought in boats from Lincolnshire, the Mayor and burgesses applied to King Edward III for a commission with powers to consider new water supplies. The commissioners authorised the construction of a canal to bring fresh water from Anlaby springs but in 1401 water was still being carried across the Humber in boats. In 1402, however, springs at Daringham and Haltemprice were connected to the Anlaby supply, although the villagers whose fresh water supplies were thus taken were antagonistic, and filled in the canal with rubbish and stopped the flow with dams. Finally, the Mayor and burgesses requested Pope John XXIII to publish a bill of excommunication against the delinquents of Anlaby, Haltemprice and districts adjacent to Springhead, and contentions ceased after a missive from the College of Cardinals at Rome dated 20th July, 1415.

Hull was created a County by Royal Charter in 1440 and in 1447 a new Charter authorized its enlargement to include the Springhead area and so safeguard the water supply. It also gave the Corporation legal powers to purchase more springs within its new boundary and

VIII. Elm Water Pipe dug up in Hu[...]
Photography by permission of Kingston upon Hull Corporation Water Departme[...]

to construct a new canal called Spring Dyke thus affording a direct route, from the springs to the town, of approximately three-and-a-half miles. When Spring Dyke was completed, a moat called Bush Dyke was constructed at its termination, which acted as a reservoir for the Hull inhabitants who could collect water from it in buckets. (The Bush Dyke was filled in in 1775, but is still shown on Bower's map of 1786 seen in Plate VII).

In about 1460 a system of lead pipes, connected to Bush Dyke reservoir, were laid in some of the streets by a Hull merchant, Sir William Knowles, enabling inhabitants to set up manual pumps in their houses if they wanted to draw water from this first mains system. However, Jones (1955) records that this system was unsuccessful for the pipes were soon removed. Thus, for more than a century and a half, street water carriers sold Bush Dyke water from their carts until the first Water Company was formed in 1616. This company used a horse-operated pump to raise fresh water from Spring Dyke to the cistern constructed on top of a warehouse built at the corner of Waterhouse Lane. These waterworks are shown on Bower's plan (Plate VII). The company laid the first wooden pipes, consisting of bored out elm trunks, one end being tapered to fit into the end of another trunk (see Plate VIII). A water rate was paid to the Company by those who had a supply laid into their houses, but poorer inhabitants could obtain a supply from public water points.

The Corporation leased the waterworks in 1773 to a Mr. Wright, who installed a primitive steam engine to replace the horse pump. This engine was unable to cope with the increasing demands for water and was replaced by a more powerful engine in 1779. Between 1775 and 1790 the number of people paying water rates doubled, and mains were extended to supply growing residential areas with water twice per week. Also an order was issued for cleansing, covering and fencing off that portion of the Spring Dyke opposite the Infirmary, an order which caused dissatisfaction since it deprived poorer people of access to their water supply.

In 1820 a new reservoir outside the town enabled Spring Dyke water to be passed through a form of filtration before being pumped into the elevated cistern. Jones (1955) records this as possibly the earliest reference to any form of water treatment in Britain. A drought occurred in 1825 and not many years later a cholera epidemic broke out, and later a visiting health official reported that the supply of water was "... too meagre for health, cleanliness and general sanitary purposes of Hull". (Sheahan, 1865). The Corporation appointed a Water Committee in 1838, who in 1842 requested the advice of Wickstead on the potential of the Springhead source which, in 1842, was only just able to supply $2\frac{2}{3}$ g.p.h.p.d. Wickstead tested the Springhead springs and advised the Water Committee to develop a new source from the River Hull at Stoneferry.

An Act of Parliament was obtained in June 1843 for the construction of Stoneferry waterworks and the first complete supply of water was given in August 1845. River water was taken through a sluice, opened for about two hours at extreme ebb tide, into a large shallow reservoir, whence it passed through a filter and was pumped to supply via a tower at a high level. Consumers had to provide cistern storage since the supply was made available only for three hours per day to each of four districts. However, people soon objected to the muddy, salty and polluted river water, and in 1849 a second epidemic of cholera killed 1,860 people, i.e. one in forty-three of Hull's population. Following local medical advice, inhabitants were returned to the Spring Dyke source.

In 1858 Mr. William Warden of Hull offered to obtain 5,000,000 gallons of pure water per day from Springhead. He sank two 16-inch diameter bores to 252 and 400 feet respectively, and produced 2,000,000 g.p.d. without pumping, and 4,500,000 g.p.d. from a six-day pumping test in 1860. The Corporation commenced work at the site in 1861 on a well and borehole, the erection of two engines, an ornamental tower for the chimney and stand pipe, engine and boiler houses (Plate IX) and the laying of a main to Stoneferry works. The river water was shut off at Stoneferry on 29th January, 1864, before the inauguration of the engines at Springhead. During the development of the borehole and headworks at Springhead, the Spring Ditch was still used for water supply.

The Springhead source had become more fully developed by 1884 and comprised two pumping wells, with additional shafts and boreholes sunk into them, and 5,500 feet of adit. Demand for water was increasing and in 1883 the statutory water supply limits had been further extended to include Anlaby, Willerby, Kirkella and Hessle. In 1884, the Kingston upon Hull Corporation Water Act gave powers to construct works for additional water (not exceeding

50,000 g.p.d.) at Mill Dam, Cottingham. Completed in 1890, the pumping station (Plate X) comprised three pumping wells, shafts, borehole, 3,250 feet of adit and three steam engines capable of pumping 3,500,000 g.p.d. each. The yield from a pumping test at Mill Dam in 1891 was 6,250,000 g.p.d.

The Newington Water Company had been formed in 1874 to supply an area of six to seven square miles to the west of Hull, including the village of Swanland and parts of Ferriby. Between 25,000 and 30,000 people consumed about 900,000 g.p.d., the supply being obtained from two 9½-foot diameter wells, 65 feet deep, with two 20-inch diameter boreholes of 245 feet and 120 feet depth respectively at Swanland Pumping Station. This source became salty and the Company applied in 1893 to construct new works at Dunswell. Although this application was unsuccessfully opposed by Hull Corporation, the latter finally purchased the Company's works in 1893 and then promptly abandoned them, supplying the population from the Springhead and Mill Dam sources. The capacity of each of the steam-driven engines at Springhead in 1900 was 5,000,000 g.p.d.

The Corporation constructed a 500,000 gallon reservoir at Raywell in 1904 and a 10,000,000 gallon covered reservoir at Keldgate in 1909. In 1911, with an increasing demand for water, authority was obtained to construct new works at Dunswell, about three miles north of Hull, to extend the statutory area of supply eastwards to include the Rural Districts of Skirlaugh and Patrington, and to supply water in bulk to Hedon, Withernsea and Hornsea. The Dunswell works commenced in 1914 but were stopped by the Treasury in the following year. Agreement was reached with Withernsea and Hedon in 1914 to supply water in bulk, and a 14½ mile main to Withernsea was completed in 1915. A water tower, consisting of two tanks was constructed in 1916, the lower tank of 300,000 gallon capacity supplying Withernsea town, while the higher tank of 100,000 gallon capacity supplied the neighbouring rural area. During the 1914-18 war, Hull Corporation supplied army camps in Holderness, e.g. at Spurn Head, Sunk Island and Paull, and in 1927 a booster station was constructed at Bilton to improve the water pressure in Holderness. In 1928 a bulk supply was given to Hornsea after the construction of a 300,000 gallon water tower on the town boundary.

Dunswell Pumping Station was finally opened in 1931 and comprised one main 16-foot diameter pumping well, 17 shafts, boreholes and 5,200 feet of adit. (During the construction of Dunswell Pumping Station, 3,900 feet of adit were constructed at Mill Dam Station in an attempt to increase the yield, but no additional water was obtained.) In 1932 a 200,000 gallon water tower was constructed at Swanland.

In order to further increase the supply of water, the Corporation obtained powers in 1930 to construct wells, bores and adits at Kelleythorpe, near Driffield but so onerous were the compensation requirements, that an alternative and more ambitious impounding scheme was proposed for Farndale in the North Riding. This scheme incorporated the valleys of Farndale, Rosedale and Bransdale, a gathering ground of 16,000 acres, and involved the construction of a 6,000,000,000 gallon storage reservoir in Farndale itself (which is floored by impervious shales of the Lower Lias series) impounding the River Dove, with tunnels bringing the River Leven and Hodge Beck from the higher valleys of Rosedale and Bransdale on either side into the reservoir. In order to maintain a gravity supply to Keldgate reservoir at Hull, the mains would pass through a three-mile tunnel in the northern Wolds at Burdale. The estimated yield of the scheme, including compensation water was 20,000,000 g.p.d. The Corporation accordingly abandoned their 1930 Act and obtained Parliamentary powers in 1933 for the Farndale works.

Rainfall and river gauging were started between 1934 and 1937 in Farndale, Bransdale and Rosedale and a survey of the proposed headworks and the route of the 60-mile aqueduct to Hull was completed. The reliable yield of the Springhead, Mill Dam, and Dunswell underground works was 14,000,000 g.p.d. and the daily consumption at this time was 13,000,000 g.p.d. An assured water supply was essential for an expanding port and developing industries, and it was estimated that the Farndale Scheme would satisfy increasing demand for 80 years. In 1937, however, the City Council decided to defer any decision for five years, during which time the 1939-45 war occurred.

A serious water shortage was created in 1945 by increased demand and by drought conditions and a similar shortage occurred in nine of the following ten years. From November, 1945 to November, 1946 there was a maximum deficiency of 2,000,000 g.p.d. but in 1947 the

IX. Original Design for Springhead Water Works by Thomas Dale, 18
Photography by permission of Kingston upon Hull Corporation Water Departme

Minister of Health informed the Corporation that regardless of their soft water requirements for use in industry, there was no prospect of the Farndale Scheme being sanctioned for at least five years. Thus the Corporation must adopt a short-term policy from a nearer and cheaper source.

A borehole was sunk at Aike in 1948 but water was found only in small quantities and this was hard and ferruginous. Between July, 1947 and December, 1950 the maximum deficiency was 3,000,000 g.p.d. and the position was further aggravated in 1948 when Beverley Borough requested a bulk supply after their borehole source had become polluted. 2,900 feet of new adit at Dunswell Pumping Station, were completed in December, 1953 but no additional water was obtained and between December, 1952 and October, 1954 the maximum deficiency of supply rose to 4,500,000 g.p.d. In 1946 the Corporation had applied to the Ministry of Health, under Section 14 of the 1945 Water Act, to ensure that further abstractions from the chalk would be controlled. The greatest number of boreholes were being sunk in the vicinity of Mill Dam, Cottingham and Dunswell Pumping Stations, where the market gardening industry was developing rapidly and private abstraction was having a detrimental effect on the yields of both pumping stations. The South East Yorkshire Area (Conservation of Water) Order, protecting the central portion of the county from the coast between Flamborough and Hornsea, west to Driffield and south to the Humber, and including Beverley and Hull, became effective from 9th March, 1949. Between 1950 and 1961, 15 applications for licences for new boreholes were made, 11 of which were opposed by the Corporation Water Department. After Ministry Inquiries, however, nine of these 11 received a licence and two (made in 1961) did not. It would thus appear that the Order did not benefit the Corporation until 1961.

A further attempt to conserve water in Hull was made by intensive waste detection work by the Corporation. Before the introduction of a waste detection system in 1932, domestic and unmetered consumption was 33 g.p.h.p.d. Constant night sounding and house-to-house inspection reduced this figure to 25 g.p.h.p.d., and the city area was divided into 42 waste detection districts.

Demand for water still increased and the daily average demand had risen to 18,000,000 g.p.d. against the reliable dry-weather yield of the three pumping stations of 14,000,000 g.p.d. Restrictions on capital expenditure prevented the implementation of the 1933 Act, and efforts to increase yields from the chalk by constructing a new borehole at Aike and adits at Dunswell had failed. In 1949 the Corporation began to gauge the upper and non-tidal reaches of the River Hull, with the possibility of obtaining a cheap, industrial, non-potable water supply and thereby relieving the demand on the general supply. By 1953 no appreciable additional water had been obtained after an expenditure of over £100,000 and the Farndale Scheme was still out of the question owing to cost and the time factor.

Under Sections 23 and 26 of the 1945 Water Act, and Section 3 of the 1948 Water Act, the Kingston upon Hull Water Order, 1954 was obtained to allow an abstraction of 12,000,000 g.p.d. from the River Hull. Twenty objections were considered at a Public Inquiry but all were over-ruled, except for that by a Beverley ship-building firm. In this case the Corporation agreed to stop abstraction for two or three days per month, to allow the shipyard to launch vessels, if requested to do so. The final Statutory Order was obtained in July, 1955, but so serious had the water supply position become in March, 1955 that the Water Department banned the use of mains water through hosepipes for watering gardens and washing private cars. Work started on the Hempholme site for the River Hull Abstraction Scheme in February, 1956.

The Statutory Water Order, 1955 authorized two intakes, one on the West Beck tributary and the other immediately upstream of Hempholme Lock and limited abstraction from the River Hull to 15,000,000 g.p.d. (27·9 cusecs) so long as the remaining flow was not in excess of 35,000,000 g.p.d. (65·1 cusecs); up to 25,000,000 g.p.d. so long as the remaining flow did not exceed 50,000,000 g.p.d. (93·01 cusecs); and any amount could be abstracted if the flow exceeded 50,000,000 g.p.d. Gauging records at Hempholme lock indicated a maximum flow of 500,000,000 g.p.d. (930·1 cusecs); a minimum of 15,000,000 g.p.d. (27·9 cusecs) and an average flow of 90,000,000 g.p.d. at this lock. The scheme comprised the abstraction, storage and treatment of 12,000,000 g.p.d. and the construction of a 36-inch diameter trunk main from Hempholme, a distance of 16½ miles to Saltend on the eastern side of Hull. The supply would serve Holderness and the eastern part of the city.

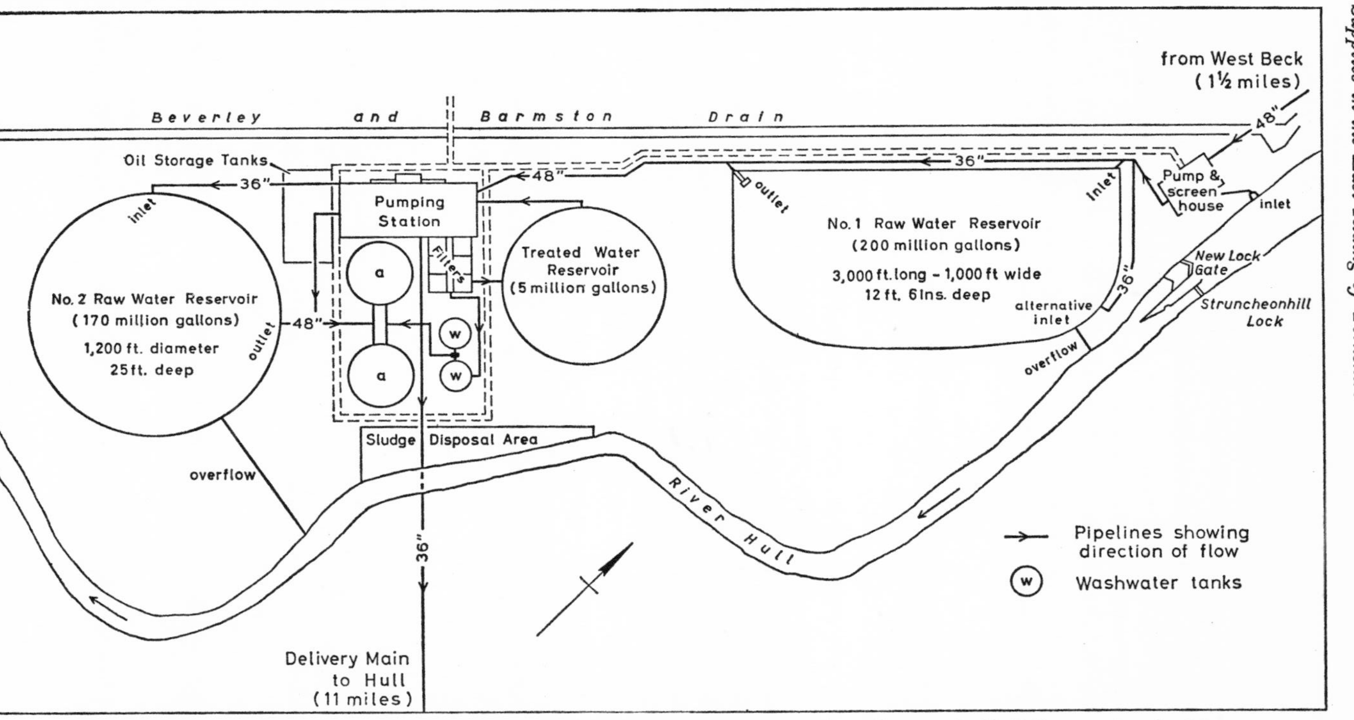

FIG. 4. DIAGRAM OF RIVER HULL (TOPHILL LOW) ABSTRACTION SCHEME. Based on diagram in Hull Corporation (1960). Accelators shown by symbol a.

A booster station had already been constructed at Patrington to improve the existing supply from underground sources to Spurn Head, Easington and part of Sunk Island, and in 1949 a water tower of 31,000 gallon capacity had been erected at Out Newton on the coast to improve storage and pressures in this south-eastern part of Holderness. In 1956 a water tower of 50,000 gallon capacity was constructed at Easington.

The old Hempholme Lock was replaced by tilting weirs (see Figure 4). Water from the two intakes flows to the pump and screen house where debris is removed, and the water chlorinated and is then pumped to the two raw water reservoirs. When the second of these is full, the top three feet of water are drawn off through the treatment plant, filters, and into the treated water reservoir, and thence pumped into the 36-inch diameter delivery main to Hull. The entire headworks are controlled from a room in the main building where control panels record river flows, intake rates, flow through the works, reservoir levels, dosage of chlorine and operation of pumps. The first water from the River Hull Abstraction Scheme (now referred to as the Tophill Low Scheme) was pumped to Hull on 3rd July, 1959. Since the river water is largely derived from chalk springs, it is similar in character to that of Hull's underground supplies, having an average hardness of 220 p.p.m., and can, therefore, be mixed with water from boreholes.

During the construction of the Tophill Low Scheme from 1956 to 1959 the Corporation improved distribution and storage within their existing network of mains. A 1956 Water Order gave powers to abstract 1,250,000 g.p.d. from a borehole at Keldgate, and an Order in 1957 authorized the construction of a 500,000 gallon reservoir off Woodgates Lane. In 1958 three new units of pumping plant at Springhead served a new trunk main from the Springhead Pumping Station to Elloughton and Brough. With the completion of the 500,000 gallon Ferriby Reservoir in 1959, and the Booster Station in 1961, the Swanland Pumping Station became defunct, and a supply was ensured to west Hull where demand had increased by 50% in the last 25 years.

Kingston upon Hull Corporation Water Department forms the largest water undertaking in the East Riding, with a statutory supply area of 312 square miles (see Figure 5). In 1960 a population of 400,000 was supplied and water was supplied in bulk to Beverley

X. Cottingham (Mill Dam) Waterworks, 1890

Photography by permission of Kingston upon Hull Corporation Water Department.

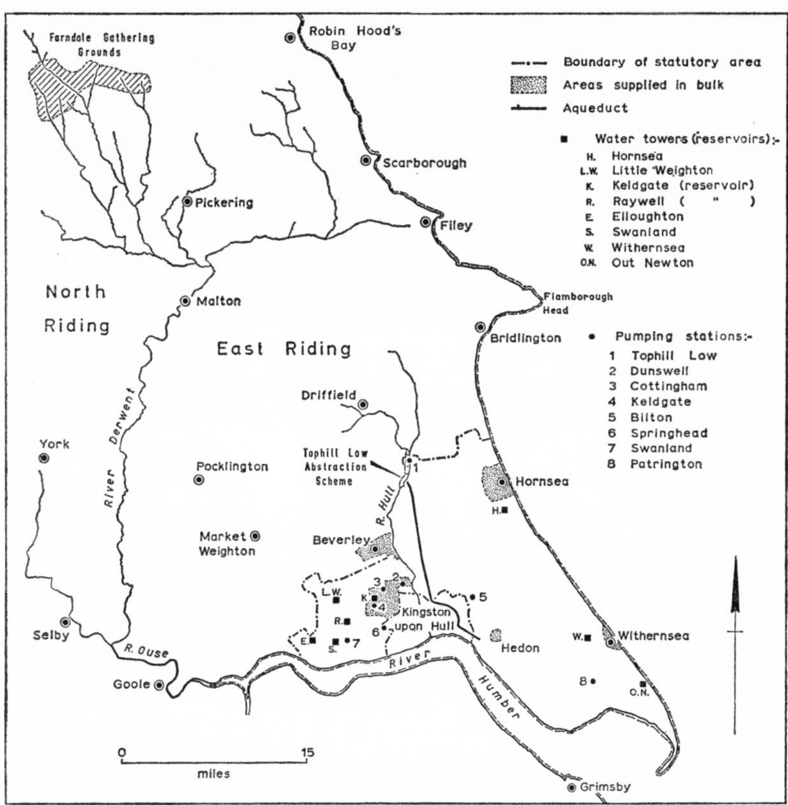

FIG. 5. STATUTORY AREA OF SUPPLY OF KINGSTON UPON HULL CORPORATION WATER DEPARTMENT.
Based on map in Hull Corporation (1960).

and Hedon, to part of Haltemprice and to Hornsea and Withernsea (as previously mentioned). The average consumption was 20,000,000 g.p.d. with 15,000,000 g.p.d. available as dry weather yield from underground sources, 12,000,000 g.p.d. being obtained from the River Hull, leaving a surplus available for future development of 7,000,000 g.p.d.

The Kingston upon Hull Water Order provided that from 1st October, 1963, Hull Corporation would take over the water authorities of Haltemprice, Beverley, Hedon, Hornsea and Withernsea and extend the limits of supply of the Corporation to include the whole of the areas of these councils not within the existing limits.

CONCLUSION

This survey has covered the entire period of growth of public water supplies in the East Riding and in Hull through to 1962 and one of the most remarkable aspects to emerge is that of the increasingly rapid growth of demand and supply during the last few decades, and the concomitant re-structuring of virtually the entire water supply industry in the area. A reminder of the scale of the comparatively recent changes which have occurred is provided by a comparison of the maps in Fig. 6, which show the pattern of statutory water supply undertakings in the East Riding in 1959 and in 1962. These two maps illustrate the contrast between the multiplicity of undertakings in 1959 and the result of amalgamations by 1st April, 1962. This re-grouping of water undertakings broadly follows the proposals made by Vail (1956) in which he included both Norton U.D. and Norton R.D. in the 'Pickering Vale area'; Bridlington, Filey and Driffield and the Rural Districts of Pocklington, Howden, Driffield and Beverley in the 'Wolds Area'; and Kingston upon Hull, Beverley, Hedon, Haltemprice, Hornsea and Withernsea in the 'Hull Area'.

It was seen earlier that, as proposed by Vail, the Norton R.D.C. water undertaking was taken over by the R. J.W.B. from 1st October, 1961 but that Norton U.D.C. preferred to remain separate, as the yield from the Howe Hill source is considered to be adequate to supply any possible future increase in demand for water.

The E.Y. (W.A.) W.B. took over those water undertakings included in Vail's Wolds Area on 1st April, 1962, and the Board's headquarters were set up in Driffield. Since its inauguration the Board has carried out mains extension schemes to new property, replaced and modified existing mains networks, and provided a mains supply to certain isolated farms and houses e.g. south-west of Middleton-on-the-Wolds, where the private supply has failed. All villages are served with a mains supply in the Board's area and only a few farms and isolated houses have their own spring or borehole supplies.

In January, 1963 the Geological Survey advised on a site for a new borehole source, possibly yielding up to 2,000,000 gallons per day in the Dalton Holme–Etton area. In February, 1963 the Board stated its policy of retaining water obtained from springs and wells on the western side of the Wolds for the Howden and Pocklington areas and of supplying Beverley R.D. from the Hutton Cranswick boreholes and the new Etton Borehole (if and when a satisfactory yield was obtained). In fact, this borehole was completed in January, 1965 and pumping tests indicated an expected regular yield of 1,750,000 g.p.d.

The discussion of water supplies in Hull showed that, as from 1st October, 1963, the Hull Corporation's statutory area of supply included all the water undertakings in Vail's Hull Area.

Finally, in the case of Derwent R.D.C., it was shown that the southern part of its statutory area was taken over by the Pontefract, Goole and Selby Water Board on 1st April, 1962 and that the northern part was taken over by the York Waterworks Company on 1st April, 1963. After the latter date, therefore, the entire Rural District was being supplied from outside the East Riding.

Thus, by the end of 1963, only three statutory water supply undertakings were using sources of water in the East Riding, namely, Norton U.D.C., the East Yorkshire (Wolds Area) Water Board, and Kingston upon Hull Corporation Water Department.

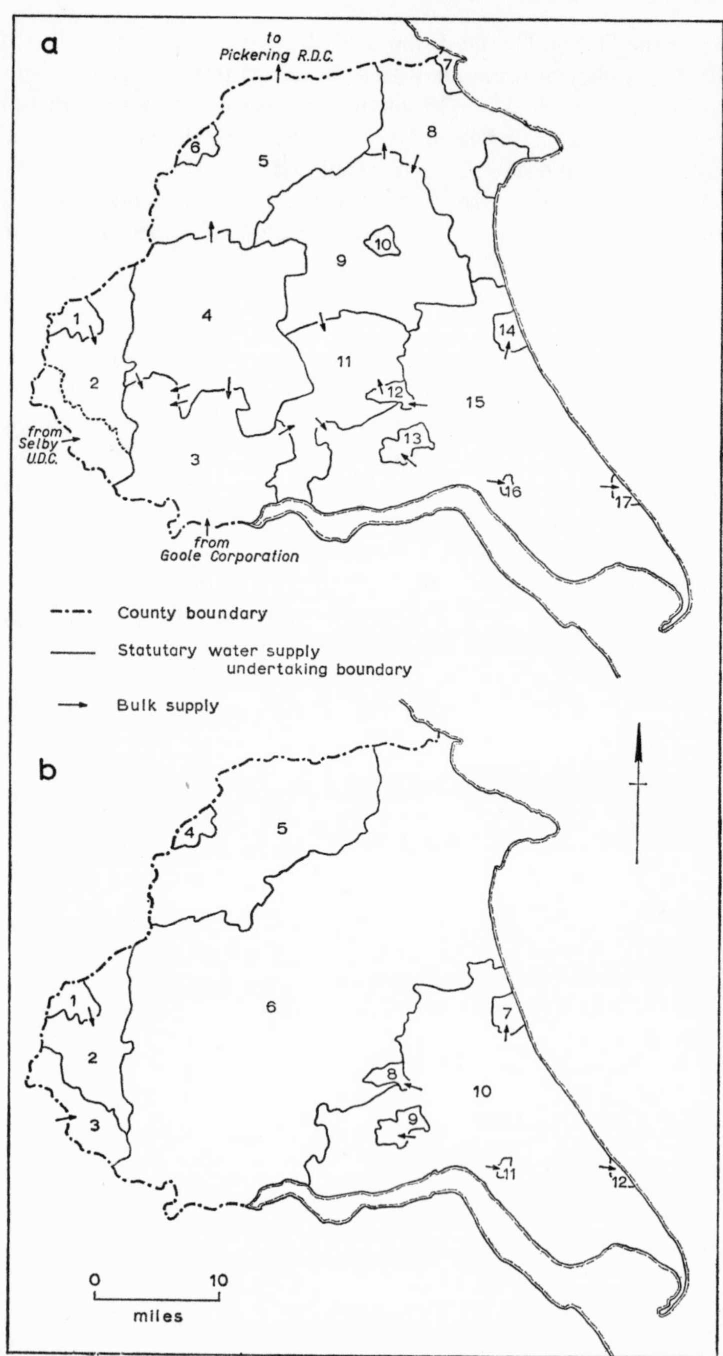
a
to
Pickering R.D.C.
1
2
3
4
5
6
7
8
9
10
11
12
13
14
15
16
17
from
Selby
U.D.C.
from
Goole Corporation
County boundary
Statutory water supply
undertaking boundary
Bulk supply
b
1
2
3
4
5
6
7
8
9
10
11
12
0
10
miles

FIG. 6. STATUTORY WATER SUPPLY UNDERTAKINGS.

(*a*) in 1959

1. York Waterworks Co.
2. Derwent R.D.C.
3. Howden R.D.C.
4. Pocklington R.D.C.
5. Norton R.D.C.
6. Norton U.D.C.
7. Filey U.D.C.
8. Bridlington Corporation Water Department.
9. Driffield R.D.C.
10. Driffield Water Co.
11. Beverley R.D.C.
12. Beverley Corporation Water Department.
13. Haltemprice U.D.C. (part).
14. Hornsea U.D.C.
15. Kingston upon Hull Corporation Water Department.
16. Hedon Corporation Water Department.
17. Withernsea U.D.C.

(*b*) in 1962

1. York Waterworks Co.
2. Derwent R.D.C.
3. Pontefract, Goole and Selby Water Board.
4. Norton U.D.C.
5. Ryedale Joint Water Board.
6. East Yorkshire (Wolds Area) Water Board.
7. Hornsea U.D.C.
8. Beverley Corporation Water Department.
9. Haltemprice U.D.C. (part).
10. Kingston upon Hull Corporation Water Department.
11. Hedon Corporation Water Department.
12. Withernsea U.D.C.

Chapter 3

The Utilization of Water Supplies for Agricultural, Industrial and Domestic Purposes

AGRICULTURAL UTILIZATION

The Public Health Act, 1936, empowered local authorities to provide a piped supply, particularly in rural areas and The Rural Water Supplies and Sewerage Acts, 1944 to 1961, made provision for grants towards the cost of water supply and sewerage schemes carried out in the rural districts. Water Acts, in 1945 and 1948, brought up to date general water legislation. All these Acts were administered by the Ministry of Housing and Local Government consulting with the Ministry of Agriculture, Fisheries and Food (M.A.F.F.) on all questions which affect agriculture. Under section 27 of the Water Act, 1945, occupiers of agricultural land have the right to ask statutory water undertakers to provide a supply and the undertakers must do so, provided that this can be done without affecting their existing obligations or probable domestic requirements.

Many farms did not receive a piped water supply until after the 1944 Act (see p. 14) when the supply for agricultural purposes was generally estimated to be $2\frac{2}{3}$ gallons per acre by Rural District Councils. This was an average quantity which assisted in the design of water supply schemes by Consulting Engineers for the water undertakings. The demand for water by farmers increased steadily, particularly where the farm had dairying interests. The Milk and Dairies Regulations of 1949 made provision for siting, ventilation, lighting, cleanliness, and layout of the dairy and cowshed, cleanliness for beasts, operator and utensils, and regulated cooling, handling, and distribution of milk. In particular, the Regulations stated that there must be a suitable and sufficient water supply on a dairy farm, and precautions must be taken against the risk of its becoming polluted and contaminated. Further Regulations of 1959 and 1960 placed dairy farmers who produced milk for human consumption under statutory obligation to register with the

M.A.F.F. and to ensure that conditions on their farms satisfied the requirements of the Milk and Dairies Regulations. Thus there was an increased demand for mains water from dairy farmers after 1950.

All farms and holdings in the East Riding which have a supply of mains water have their supply metered, so that the quarterly readings include both domestic and agricultural consumption. The M.A.F.F. used the figures included in Table 11 as the average quantity of water needed on a farm in g.p.h.p.d. in 1962. These figures refer to the use of water for general farming purposes such as washing buildings and equipment, and watering stock. Some Rural Districts instal a separate meter to farms for field tanks, but the meter for the farmhouse usually includes consumption of water in all the outbuildings. Thus consumption figures for general farming purposes in the county are included later in discussion of domestic consumption figures in Rural Districts.

TABLE 11

Consumer	Amount (g.p.h.p.d.)
Domestic consumers	25
Milch cows, drinking	15
„ „ cleaning and milk cooling	15
Dry cows and horses	10
Pigs	3
Sheep	1½

AVERAGE QUANTITIES OF WATER FOR FARM REQUIREMENTS

Source:— M.A.F.F., (1962).

The average summer (April–September) rainfall in the East Riding varies from 12 inches in Holderness, Humberside, and the southern Vale of York to over 14 inches in the central and higher Wolds whilst average potential transpiration for the same period is 16 inches. The frequency of irrigation need has been calculated to be from 7 to 8 years in 10 in south eastern Holderness, 6 to 7 years in 10 in the Humberside region, central Holderness and the southern part of the Vale of York, and 5 to 6 years in 10 in the northern Vale of York, southern Wolds and northern Plain of Holderness. The frequency of irrigation need is less than 5 years in

10 for most of the Wolds (M.A.F.F., 1962). Thus, it is evident that the county lies on the northern fringe of the area of Eastern England which benefits from irrigation. Accordingly, farmers in the county began to purchase irrigation equipment during and after the drought year of 1959, which caused loss of yield in potato and sugar beet crops and poor grass growth.

A report by the Natural Resources (Technical) Committee (1962) noted the need for irrigation of maincrop potatoes in the East Riding during July and August in 7 or 8 years in 10, and for new potatoes in May and June every year in the south western corner of the Vale of York, in 9 out of 10 years in Humberside, and south eastern Holderness, and in 8 to 9 years in 10 in the rest of the county. The installation of irrigation equipment largely depends on an accessible, cheap, and plentiful water supply, labour to move the equipment, and the full utilization of the equipment throughout the season and from year to year and on high crop values. The crops which give the largest financial returns per unit of water applied in the East Riding are early and maincrop potatoes, grassland where it is intensively utilised, as through a dairy herd, and sugar beet. The distribution of farmers known to be irrigating in 1961 can be seen in Figure 7. The vital importance of an adequate water supply for irrigation can be seen in this distribution, for there is a complete absence of irrigation on the Chalk Wolds where surface water is absent. The majority of farmers using irrigation are situated in the Vales of Pickering and York, and the Plain of Holderness and in fact the first farm known to have installed irrigation equipment, in 1957, was in the Stamford Bridge area of the Vale of York.

Irrigation is normally applied in order to restore the soil moisture content to about 80% or more of field capacity within the root zone. If too much water is applied the surplus runs off and is wasted, and there is a danger of waterlogging and leaching of plant nutrients. In theory, irrigation is carried out when the average moisture content in the top 12 inches of the soil stands between 25% and 50% of field capacity. In practice, farmers tend to assess the soil moisture content by inspection, knowing the variable soil types and depths in each field and the root depths of the crops being grown, and by observing the appearance of plants; very few use more precise methods involving the measurement of either rainfall, or soil moisture content itself.

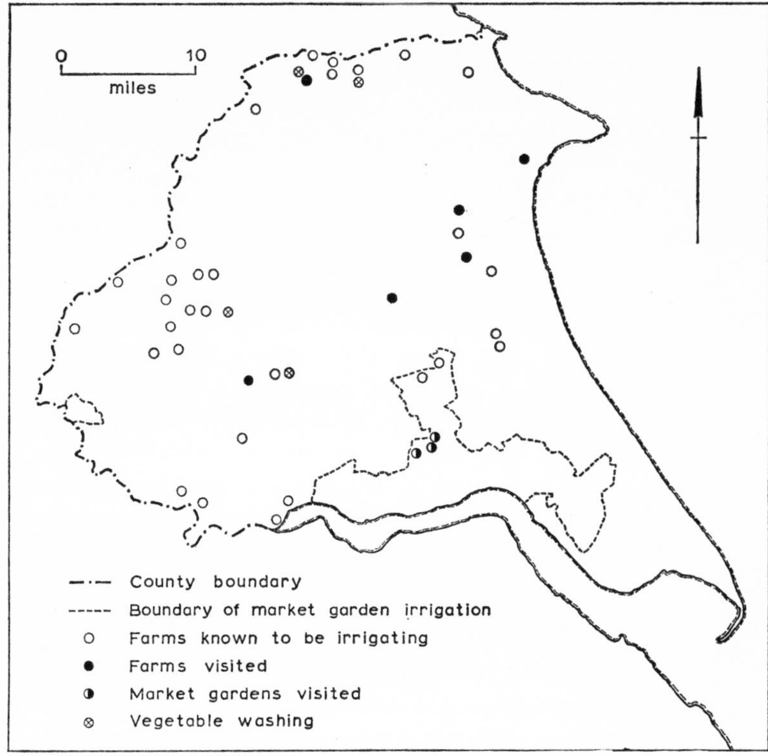

FIG. 7. DISTRIBUTION OF FARM AND HORTICULTURAL IRRIGATION IN 1961.

All the irrigators included in Figure 7 used the same type of portable, aluminium alloy mains pipeline, lateral mains and sprinklers, with a tractor-mounted pump to provide the supply of water, although each irrigation system was specifically designed to take account of the area to be irrigated, water supply sources, cropping plans, type and quality of labour available for moving equipment, soil texture, structure, profile and water-holding capacity, infiltration rate, root zone depth and the climatic conditions of the farm. The capital outlay for the portable equipment assuming a free water supply was an average of £2 7*s.* 0*d.* per acre. In fact, all the farms visited, except No. 3*, obtained a free water

*In order to protect confidential sources of information, irrigating farms are referred to only by number.

supply from ditches, the farmers being riparian owners. In most cases a temporary dam is erected in the ditch adjacent to the field to be irrigated, the ditch forming the only storage of water. An exception to this was Farm No. 2 where spring water is pumped into two marl pits which have been over-deepened to hold ½ m.g. each (Plate II), and into three smaller marl ponds of 700,000 g. capacity. In addition, by operating sluice gates on drainage dikes at appropriate times, water storage can be provided from which to irrigate adjacent fields.

Undoubtedly, the quantity of water applied to the land during any year varies considerably, and in any case, no farmer visited metered the water obtained from the stream or ditch. All the farmers applied water at the rate of 22·61 g. per acre, or equivalent to 1 inch of rain per acre, but the number of applications varied. It is doubtful whether any of the farmers in the county who were irrigating in 1961, would find it economic to do so without the free supply of water. If there is a rapid increase in the number of farmers irrigating in the county, then storage of water will be a necessity, and would increase the cost of irrigation.

In addition to the water consumed for general farming purposes and for irrigation, three vegetable-washing plants use water. The distribution of these concerns is also shown in Figure 7. Farm No. 1 started washing potatoes and carrots grown on the farm in 1958. In 1961, an average of 15 tons of potatoes were washed per day from mid-September onwards prior to despatch. The quantity of water used per day was small due to a continuous re-circulation, and as it was obtained from a ditch on the farm and not metered, the actual quantity was not known. A small quantity of mains water was used for rinsing. Carrots were washed from September to March and the water supply was taken entirely from the ditch source. The second vegetable-washing concern at Market Weighton in the Vale of York, used 300 g.p.d. of mains water in 1961 for washing an average of 10 tons of carrots per day from November to February, or until the crop finished. It is not known when this concern started vegetable washing, but it had used a large quantity of water from Market Weighton Beck and marl ponds to irrigate potatoes, sugar beet and ley grassland from 1944. The third and largest vegetable-washing concern, at Melbourne in the Vale of York, dates from January 1962, when a company composed of about 30 farmers, started to wash vegetables produced by themselves. Approximately 2,000 g.p.d. of mains water was used for an output of up to 200 tons of potatoes and carrots per week. Here, again, the quantity of water used was small due to continuous re-circulation of water to the washing machine.

Horticulture may require up to 100 times more water per acre than does agriculture. Overhead sprinkler irrigation is common in glasshouses on market gardens, as the method is well adapted to light applications of water for the purposes of seed bed preparation, seed germination and transplanting and thinning of seedlings. In the East Riding, overhead watering by spray lines is used on lettuces planted in early January in the unheated Dutch light structures. Three or four heavy waterings, including the initial flooding before planting, are given, plus several light waterings given in sunny periods to cool the plants and prevent excessive transpiration. The lettuces are then succeeded by tomatoes in April. As the Dutch light structures and other glass-houses exclude any natural rainfall, soil moisture deficits must be made up entirely by irrigation.

The distribution of the main market gardening areas in the county is shown in Figure 7. The main, and oldest, centre of horticulture is in Haltemprice, between Cottingham (on heavy clays), Woodmansey (on light loams) and Thearne. This is the most important area in the British Isles for the production of lettuce, tomatoes and cauliflowers using the Dutch, unheated glasshouse and frames. The main influence in the use of these structures came from Dutch immigrants between 1932 and 1936. The Howden area was an overspill region from Cottingham for Dutch growers who grew tomatoes and lettuce under glass, cauliflowers and bulbs outside, and fruit trees. In 1960, there were approximately 100 acres of pears in this region, though this horticultural area is not shown on Figure 7. On the sands between York, Riccall and Cawood, salad crops are grown under Dutch lights. A smaller region of horticulture lies to the east of Hull on mixed soils derived from the Boulder Clay between Hedon and Thorngumbald. Here English glass structures are more common than Dutch lights, and mixed crops with flowers and hot-house plants are grown for distant markets. The light sands between South Cave, Brough, Elloughton and Welton on Humberside are becoming increasingly important for the production of lettuce, and tomatoes under glass, celery, cauliflowers, leeks and some flowers.

In 1950, there were approximately 193 separate holdings (total acreage 6,800) in the Cottingham–Beverley market gardening area to the west of the River Hull, of which 90% were used for intensive crop growing. A large part of their acreage was covered with glass-houses, both permanent and movable. Dutch glass-houses and Dutch lights and the acreage covered by glass have increased every year since 1950. Almost every holding had a borehole for water supply which had been sunk since the 1930s. The average depth of the bore-holes, of which 73 were in use in this area in 1950, was 90 feet, and they varied in diameter from 2 inches to 12 inches. It has been estimated that in 1950 a total quantity of 100 m.g. per annum (m.g.a.) was obtained from the 73 boreholes although it is very difficult to obtain quantities of water used by growers during any one year for irrigation, because few records are kept of hours of pumping from the boreholes.

However, as an approximation it is usually assumed (M.A.A.F., 1962) that growers apply 0·25 m.g. per acre before planting lettuce; 11·25 m.g. were applied in the 1950 season, but this figure has naturally increased since then. Tomatoes grown under glass require 1 inch per acre per week for 20 weeks during growth, and lettuce requires ½ inch per acre per week for 16 weeks during growth. Total requirements for some crops grown outside where the amount of irrigation is so variable are shown in Table 12.

TABLE 12

Crop	Pre-planting requirement (inches)	Requirement during growing period (inches)	Length of growing period (months)
Cabbages	2	16	4
Sprouts	2	22	12
Peas	6	12	3
Cauliflowers	3	18	various

WATER REQUIREMENT FOR HORTICULTURAL CROPS GROWN OUTSIDE

In 1950, the largest user of water in the Cottingham area had six boreholes with an extraction rate of 14,000 g.p.h. and used a total of 19½ m.g. in 1949. It can thus be seen that there may be serious financial implications if the grower's own borehole supply diminishes and mains water must be obtained. This is particularly so in the case of watercress, where one Cottingham grower with a large acreage supplies 16 m.g. per annum of water to his cress beds, at a constant temperature, from a borehole of 2,800 g.p.h. rated capacity which is run for 24 hours per day for eight months of the year. With mains water the cost of watercress growing would be prohibitive.

Until Hull Corporation augmented its water resources by abstraction from the River Hull in 1959, it was unable to supply large quantities of mains water to growers, who therefore had to use their private borehole sources for domestic supplies. Since 1960, however, more growers have installed mains water for both domestic consumption and for irrigation on the holdings. Although this latter use is so expensive, it has proved impossible to obtain a licence to construct a borehole in the Cottingham area since 1960 due to the implementation of the South East Yorkshire Area (Conservation of Water) Order 1949 designed to prevent the area being over-pumped (see p. 47).

It is difficult to determine total quantities of water used in irrigation from the data collected. Detailed "Irrigation Scheme Record" sheets are completed by each grower for the M.A.F.F. which contain details of acreage, crops grown, water requirements, source of water, storage, and areas irrigated in any one season, and from which it would obviously be possible to estimate both the total daily and seasonal maximum requirements for water on the holdings in the East Riding. Unfortunately access to these records is not permitted. Some general guide, however, is given by the fact that in 1960 the Geological Survey and Museum provided data to Hull Corporation Water Department showing that abstractions by private borehole users were 4·4 m.g.d. and as the Geological Survey received returns for abstractions of only 50,000 g.p.d. upwards, the Corporation estimated that the total abstraction by private borehole users in their statutory area (in the vicinity of Hull) in 1960 was at least 5 m.g.d. It is still not possible to assess from this figure the quantity of water used by horticultural consumers, however, as the figure includes abstraction from boreholes by industrial consumers as well.

DOMESTIC AND INDUSTRIAL UTILIZATION

Section 31 of the Third Schedule of the Water Act 1945, states that water undertakers in England and Wales "shall provide in their mains and communication pipes a supply of wholesome water sufficient for the domestic purposes of all owners and occupiers of premises within the limits of supply who under the special Act are entitled to demand a supply for those purposes".

Table 13 shows the average consumption of water for domestic purposes in 1949 in the East Riding as reported by Waters (1949). It can be seen from Table 13 that domestic consumption was lower in 'city' areas than in 'urban' areas as the proportions of baths and water closets in city areas per dwelling was lower than in urban areas, where more modern residential development was taking place in the post-war years. Between 1935 and 1949 the domestic and unmetered consumption in city areas supplied in detail by Hull, increased by 6% to 30%. This increase could not be more closely specified due to the absence of knowledge of wastage in 1935. Slum clearance and better sanitation in new houses accounted for the increasing consumption and Hull Corporation envisaged a future consumption of 10·5 m.g.d. for 350,000 people (that is at 30 g.p.h.p.d.) in the statutory area of supply supplied in detail. Those urban areas supplied in bulk by Hull Corporation and discussed in Chapter 2, estimated a future consumption of 40 g.p.h.p.d. for domestic purposes, which represented an increase of 23·5% over the 1949 figure of 32·4 g.p.h.p.d. Thus the future domestic demand for 40,000 people at 40 g.p.h.p.d. would be 1·6 m.g.d., and allowing for trade usage would total 2·0 m.g.d.

The average consumption in rural areas in 1949 can be seen from Table 13 to be 30 g.p.h.p.d. including farm supplies. In all the rural districts the consumption of water was increasing due to the extension of mains networks and improved sanitation. Also national policies being directed towards intensified agricultural production, with raised standards of health for cattle and other animals, were increasing the demands for water for agricultural use. After 1950, slow progress began to be made in the provision of sewerage facilities in the Rural Districts which had hitherto been almost non-existent. Even in March 1957, however, the Pollution Officer of the then Yorkshire Ouse R.B. remarked that progress in schemes of sewerage and sewage disposal was slow due to recurrent restrictions on capital expenditure in the post-war years. Economy measures on the part of Rural Districts included the preparation and subsequent shelving of schemes, so that consumption of water in the villages was slowed down to a certain extent. Building development in villages without adequate sewerage facilities was limited.

TABLE 13

Areas supplied	Domestic consumption in g.p.h.p.d.
'City' areas (supplied by Hull Corporation in detail)	24·8
'Urban' areas (supplied by Hull Corporation in bulk)	32·4
Driffield and Norton Urban Districts	30·2
'Urban' areas as a whole	32·0
'Rural' areas (including farm supplies)	29·9

AVERAGE DOMESTIC CONSUMPTION IN THE EAST RIDING, 1949

The 1951 Census revealed that 55% of private households in the county had exclusive use of all five of the household arrangements covered by the census questions, and a further 16% had all except a fixed bath. (The corresponding figures for England and Wales as a whole were 53% and 20% respectively). Twenty per cent of households were without the exclusive use of a piped water supply, which was higher than the 17% for the whole of England and Wales. The figure for the East Riding of 14% of households in undivided occupations entirely without piped water, was more than twice as high as that for the whole country, the incidence being highest in the more rural areas remote from Hull, York and the coastal towns. The Rural Districts of Driffield, Norton, and Howden had 46%, 34% and 30% respectively of households without piped supplies. It was noted in early discussions (see p. 14) that Driffield and Norton had suffered the greatest decline in population between the 1931 and 1951 census dates, due to the remoteness of Wolds farms and villages, many of which received mains water as late as the 1960s.

Data on water supply and household arrangements included in the 1961 Census and in Table 14, are not directly comparable with those in the 1951 Census discussed above. Instead of a piped water supply, the 1961 Census discussed a cold and hot water tap supply. Thus in 1961, 157,853 or 94·6% of all households in the East Riding had exclusive use of a cold water tap in the building, 2,055 or 1·2% shared, and 6,979 or 4·2% were entirely without the use of a cold water tap. Since 1951 the proportion of households of all sizes and occupations without a cold water tap fell from 13·5% to 4·2% and the proportion with only shared use fell from 6·9% to 1·2%. Thus a considerable improvement in the piping of a water supply into houses took place between 1951 and 1961 and this contributed towards the increasing consumption of water. Similar improvements were noted in the exclusive use of a hot water tap in the building by 123,633 households or 74·1% in the county, 1,714 or 1·0% sharing, and 41,540 or 24·9% without the use of a hot water tap, and 120,075 or 71·9% of households with exclusive use of a fixed bath, 3,425 or 2·1% with shared use, and 43,387 or 26·0% entirely without a fixed bath in the building. From 1951 to 1961 the proportion of households entirely without access to a bath decreased from 38·0% to 26·0%, reflecting the modernisation of property and new building development, both producing an increasing demand for water. 90·9% or 151,706 households had exclusive use of a W.C., 3,681 or 2·2% had shared use, and 11,500 or 6·9% of households were without the use of a W.C. It is difficult to assess the increase in consumption of water from these figures since the W.C. can be emptying into a main sewer, septic tank, or cesspool. Occasionally, a practical limitation exists on the amount of flushing of a W.C. emptying into a cesspool where, for example, the cesspool is of limited capacity.

The total population of 510,904 in the county at the 1951 Census indicated a net increase, between 1931 and 1951, of about 28,000 people, which, taking the longer time interval into account showed a retarded rate of increase (5·8%) as compared with the corresponding increase of 4·8% in the previous decade of 1921 to 1931. Between 1951 and 1961 the population of the East Riding increased by 16,388, representing a rate of 0·31% a year, compared with a rate of 0·28% a year between 1931 and 1951. A loss of population in the county between 1951 and 1961 due to migration was outweighed by the natural increase in population. The population of Kingston-upon-Hull and the other towns increased between 1951 and 1961 and in the Rural Districts of Beverley and Holderness, especially in those parishes adjoining Kingston-upon-Hull. The decline in population in the Rural Districts of Bridlington, Driffield, Norton and Pocklington in the same period continued the earlier trend already noted. It is important to note the lack of household arrangements in these rural areas (see Table 12) especially in Driffield R.D., which is reflected in the low percentage of households having exclusive use of all four arrangements in the last column of Table 14.

Vail commented in 1956 on the difficulty of knowing the exact figure of average consumption for all purposes in the county, as some water undertakings had no means of measuring water passed into supply. He considered an average consumption of 48 g.p.h.p.d. was a reasonable figure for the population supplied with mains in 1955. Domestic consumption was particularly high in the seaside resorts, based on the resident population, which can be seen in Table 15. Factors affecting water consumption in the county in 1955 were, firstly, a water shortage in the Hull area, when pressures were reduced to minimize losses so that consumption was being kept down artificially until 1959. Secondly, waste detection was poor in most of the Rural Districts and, until the 1960s, was entirely neglected in some remote areas. Some water in the lowland areas of the county was very acid and aggressive to metals and where the pH was not corrected, the mains and services became corroded and therefore produced leakage. This problem was still prevalent in some rural areas in the 1960s. In the fairly level Vales of York and Pickering and the Plain of Holderness, the laying of distribution mains was simple but the absence of suitable sites for local storage reservoirs meant the installation of heavy pipes and fittings was required, or the provision of pressure-reducing valves. Sometimes high pressures were adopted to economize on the size of mains when local storage reservoirs would have been better. In the Wolds, distribution of water from one valley to another frequently involved high pressures but supply by gravity was used along each valley. As previously mentioned, the consumption in the county, particularly in the Rural Districts, was increasing mainly because of improvement of sanitary fittings when houses were modernised, and improvement in standards of personal hygiene.

The increase in population and consumption of water between 1948 and 1955 discussed by Waters and Vail can be seen in Table

15, with the 1961 Census population figures and average consumption in 1961 analysed from the records of the statutory water undertakings. Vail stressed the difficulty in forecasting with any accuracy the consumption of water per head in 25 to 30 years' time (i.e. 1985). He allowed for improved waste detection, renewal of corroded mains, provision of piped supplies to isolated areas, improved sanitation with new or modernised housing, and allowed 35 g.p.h.p.d. for domestic (unmetered) supplies in urban areas and 30 g.p.h.p.d. in rural areas (due to slower modernisation of property). Industrial requirements he assessed on the 1955 demand and probable developments, but he was most conservative in his assessment of agricultural requirements, for he allowed the same consumption for stock as had Waters (1949). Vail's estimates for 1985 are included in Table 15. He estimated the average requirements of both the North and East Ridings in 1985 would be over 46·5 m.g.d. and peak demands over 55 m.g.d. He considered that sources in 1956 should give all the water needed during the coming 30 years provided arrangements could be made for the passing of local surpluses to other areas in need. The three water undertakings carrying out this suggestion in the county from the 1940s under their 'Co-ordination Scheme', namely the Rural Districts of Howden, Beverley, and Pocklington, were discussed earlier (p. 37). Since the fairly recent amalgamation of water undertakings there has been much greater co-operation between newly-formed Joint Water Boards in sharing surpluses of water in the county.

It can be seen from Table 15 that Vail was very conservative in his estimates of population in 1985 for some authorities, notably Howden R.D. and Pocklington R.D., which had exceeded his 1985 population estimate in 1961, both authorities showing a considerable increase in average consumption between 1955 and 1961.

An anticipated deficit by 1985 of some 2,125,000 g.p.d. is shown in Table 15 for Beverley, Hedon, Haltemprice, Hornsea and Withernsea. All these authorities receive bulk supplies from Hull Corporation who calculate that their surplus to requirements in 1985 will be 2,600,000 g.p.d. This surplus would only just meet the anticipated deficit of the other five undertakings, so that Hull Corporation would be obliged to increase their abstraction from the River Hull.

Under the provisions of Section 27 of the Water Act, 1945, "statutory water undertakers supplying water other than in bulk shall give a supply of water on reasonable terms and conditions for purposes other than domestic purposes to the owner or occupier of any premises within their limits of supply who requests them to give such a supply to those premises". This use of water for trade or industrial purposes is either true 'consumption' of water when the water is eliminated from the resources of an area of supply, or water 'usage' when a quantity of water is taken from the source of supply to be re-circulated and some or all is returned to supply. The trade supply is invariably metered by the water undertaking. Most factories and other industrial premises require a potable supply from the public mains for the needs of their employees for washing, drinking, canteens, etc. In addition, water is required for manufacturing purposes and need not necessarily be a potable supply. It was seen earlier that industries in several East Riding towns had a mains supply and a private borehole supply, particularly in Barlby in Derwent R.D., and in Driffield, Bridlington, Beverley, and Hull. (The average consumption for employees in factories and offices is between 10 and 15 g.p.h.p.d.)

WATER UTILIZATION IN THE COASTAL RESORTS

The development of the coastal towns of Filey, Bridlington, Hornsea and Withernsea, as popular seaside resorts, particularly in this century, is reflected in Fig. 8 which shows the increasing annual consumption of water in the four resorts for the period during which records are available. The Withernsea data are available from the first bulk supply provided in 1916 by Hull Corporation, and similarly the Hornsea data are available from 1928 when the first bulk supply was provided. (Both these undertakings are therefore included in the bulk supply graph in Figure 13). Records of consumption in Filey were available only from 1941 and in Bridlington from 1946. Annual consumption in Withernsea increased steadily from 3·7 m.g. in 1916 to 69·9 m.g. in 1961, and increased in Hornsea from 48·3 m.g. in 1928, to 82·4 m.g. in 1961. There was an overall increase in annual consumption in Filey from 162·8 m.g. in 1941 to 186·9 m.g. in 1961 but the high consumption shown in Figure 8 in 1942 was due to increased demand for service establishments. Figure 8 shows the most erratic graph of annual consumption for Bridlington, but there was an overall increase from

340·5 m.g. in 1947 to 465·5 m.g. in 1961. The most rapid increase occurred after 1949 when the resort was developing rapidly, and because of the extension of mains water to the Rural District. The average consumption and increasing population of all four resorts are shown in Table 15.

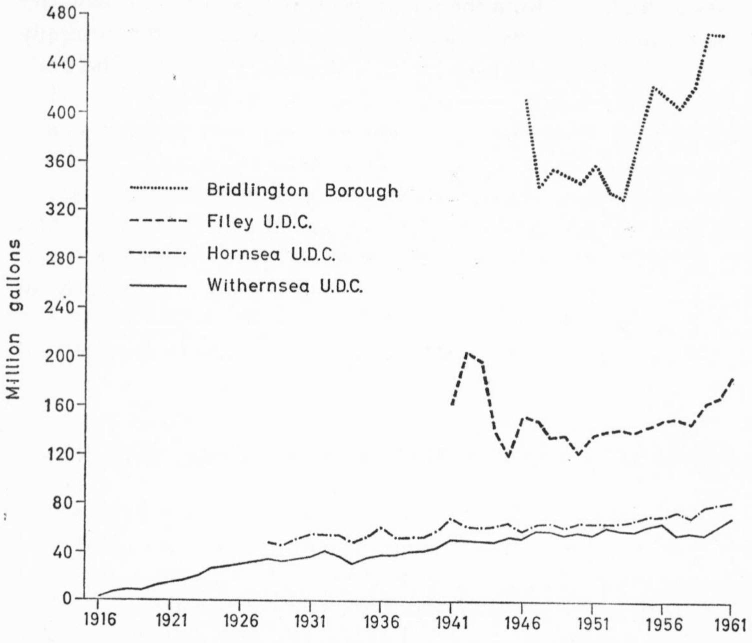

FIG. 8. ANNUAL CONSUMPTION OF WATER IN THE COASTAL RESORTS, 1916–61. Based on data supplied by U.D.C. and Borough water undertakings.

Graphs of quarterly consumption in the four resorts in Figure 9(a), and the data included in Table 16, show the considerable increase in demand in the summer season (July to September quarter) by the holiday visitors, particularly in Filey and Bridlington. This seasonal pattern of consumption in the coastal resorts can be seen in Figure 9(b), (c) and (d). In all the resorts the domestic (unmetered) demand is in excess of the trade (metered) demand. This can be seen from the consumption figures for Filey from 1959 to 1961 shown in Table 17. The domestic demand is from private houses and some hotels, while the trade demand is for schools, hospitals, shops, garages, and laundry and amenities for the

TABLE 16

Year	Quarter	Quarterly Consumption in m.g.			
		Withernsea U.D.	Hornsea U.D.	Bridlington Borough	Filey U.D.
1959	March	8·9*	17·5	102·2	22·8
	June	15·6	19·7	116·3	42·6
	September	16·8	22·4	142·5	64·8
	December	14·3	18·3	106·3	33·3
	Total	55·6	77·9	467·3	613·5
1960	March	13·5	17·4	101·3	26·6
	June	15·5	22·7	117·9	42·5
	September	18·0	22·3	143·5	67·0
	December	15·2	18·7	104·6	32·0
	Total	62·2	81·1	467·3	168·1
1961	March	14·9	19·0	106·6	33·0
	June	17·2	21·2	121·5	49·7
	September	19·5	23·0	133·4	71·6
	December	18·3	19·2	104·0	32·6
	Total	69·9	82·4	465·5	186·9

QUARTERLY CONSUMPTION OF WATER IN THE COASTAL RESORTS, 1959-61
*One month missing in records

TABLE 17

Year	Domestic Consumption (1,000 gallons)	Metered Consumption (1,000 gallons)	Total Consumption (1,000 gallons)
1959	113,653	49,816	163,469
1960	117,169	51,008	168,177
1961	128,097	58,762	186,859

ANNUAL CONSUMPTION OF WATER IN FILEY U.D. 1959-1961

summer visitors such as the golf course, putting green, bowling green, boating pool, and caravan sites. These metered supplies are typical of all four of the resorts, but Bridlington has a trading estate within its boundaries where miscellaneous light industry has a metered supply.

Consumption at the Butlin's (Ltd.) holiday camp which is plotted separately in Fig. 9(b) increased from 29·4 m.g.a. in 1957 to 40·7 m.g.a. in 1961, by which date the maximum number of campers on the site was 8,000. The South Crescent Dairies was the largest metered consumer in the town of Filey, and its average annual consumption of 2·25 m.g. is also included in the trade (metered) graph.

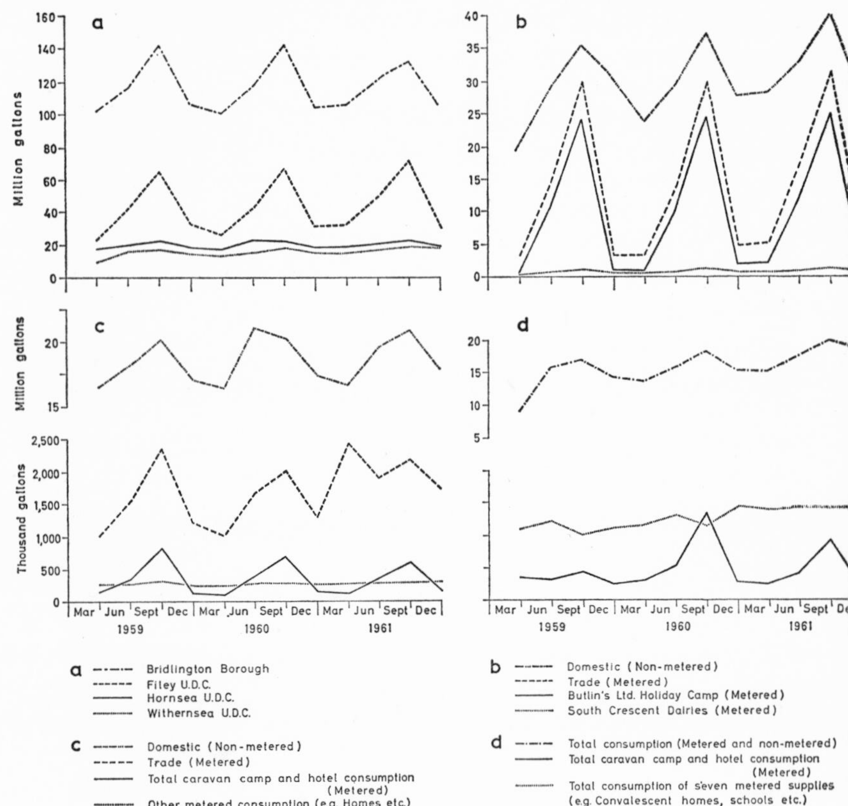

FIG. 9. QUARTERLY CONSUMPTION OF WATER (*a*) IN THE FOUR COASTAL RESORTS, 1959–61, (*b*) FILEY U.D., (*c*) HORNSEA U.D. and (*d*) WITHERNSEA U.D. Based on data supplied by U.D.C. and Borough water undertakings.

It can be seen from Figure 9(c) that domestic, trade and hotel and caravan camp (metered) demand in Hornsea also showed a peak in the July to September quarter, but demand from the hospital and

Homes showed a steady pattern throughout the year. Similarly in Figure 9(d), though the total consumption and caravan camp and hotel consumption in Withernsea showed a peak in the summer quarter, the consumption of the seven largest metered consumers showed a steady all year round pattern of consumption as they were independent of holiday visitors.

Surveys were made by the coastal towns and by Holderness R.D.C. of the distribution of caravan sites on the East Riding coast at the end of August 1960, by which time it was evident that some form of planning control was long overdue. Mayoh (1961) recorded 6,220 caravans on the East Riding coast in 1952, of which 56% were in Bridlington or on the coast to the north, 28% were on the coast from the south end of Bridlington to the south end of Hornsea and 16% were south of Hornsea. By 1958, an increase of 2,080 caravans, to 8,300 had taken place, which was equivalent to a 33·4% increase in six years. The East Riding C.C. Planning Authority had in 1958 set aside land for 80 caravans at Barmston 200 at Atwick, 1,100 at Hornsea, 450 at Tunstall, 200 at Withernsea, and 140 at Easington, stipulating a minimum distance of 15 feet between caravans in a row, 20 feet between rows, at least one lavatory per eight caravans, and the provision of a water supply, usually in the form of stand pipes. The E.R.C.C. envisaged a total of 11,144 caravan places by 1965, but, in fact, by the time of the August 1960 survey there were approximately 10,171 caravans (as well as miscellaneous bungalows, chalets, old railway coaches, etc.) and so proposals were made for the removal, as soon as practicable after the 1960 survey was completed, of sites in Filey U.D., Bridlington R.D., Bridlington Borough, Holderness R.D., and Withernsea U.D. Only the Hornsea U.D. caravan sites conformed to the E.R.C.C. requirements for spacing of caravans and sanitary facilities.

In the August 1960 caravan survey, Filey U.D. had 13 caravan sites which contained 2,908 caravans. In 1961 only three caravan sites existed, including the Primrose Valley site, all of which had shops and adequate lavatory and water supply facilities. The consumption of water on all the caravan sites in the statutory area of supply of Bridlington Corporation was assessed as 50 g. per caravan per day. In August 1960, 3,577 caravans existed in the Bridlington R.D., and 1,350 caravans in the Borough. In Hornsea in August 1960 there were 755 caravans but by 1961 there were 917.

For comparison, the total caravan camp and hotel metered consumption from 1959 to 1961 is plotted in Figure 9(c).

The survey of August 1960 showed six caravan sites in Withernsea licenced to accommodate 649 caravans. The total caravan camp and hotel consumption from 1959 to 1961 is plotted in Figure 9(d) and the total quarterly consumption in the five caravan camps and two hotels can be seen in Table 18. The increase in consumption in 1960 was due to the expansion of the Golden Sands Chalet Park after September 1959 and the improvement of the sanitary facilities on the other caravan sites.

TABLE 18

Year	Quarter	Consumption (1000 gallons)
1959	March	340
	June	321
	September	428
	December	236
	Total	1,325
1960	March	297
	June	504
	September	1,333
	December	267
	Total	2,401
1961	March	231
	June	395
	September	900
	December	166
	Total	1,692

QUARTERLY CONSUMPTION WITHERNSEA, U.D., 1959-61, (FIVE CARAVAN CAMPS AND TWO HOTELS)

From this discussion of the development of the four coastal resorts as residential towns and seaside resorts, with increasing population, as seen from the data in Table 15, it is evident that consumption of water will continue to increase and all four towns must provide adequate storage to cope with the large summer demand. As discussed in an earlier section, Filey and Bridlington

Borough are now included in the E.Y. (W.A.) W.B. and do not envisage any deficiency in water supply by 1985. Hornsea and Withernsea depend on Hull Corporation for a bulk supply and although it can be seen in Table 13 that both envisaged a deficiency in water supply by 1985, Hull Corporation plan to cope with this by increased abstraction from the River Hull.

WATER UTILISATION IN THE URBAN DISTRICTS OF DRIFFIELD AND NORTON

The increase in population between 1948 and 1961 in the two market towns of Driffield and Norton can be seen from Table 15 to be very slight in comparison with the coastal towns or with Hull. Likewise the consumption of water in both towns has remained fairly steady. Table 19 illustrates this steady pattern of average

TABLE 19

Year	Month	Lowest Consumption (1000 gallons)	Highest Consumption (1000 gallons)
1959	January	292	
	June		336
1960	June		341
	December	297	
1961	January	298	
	July		340

AVERAGE DAILY CONSUMPTION IN DRIFFIELD U.D. 1959

daily consumption in Driffield from 1959 to 1961. Consumption in each year rose from January to a peak in June 1959 and 1960, and July in 1961. Figure 10 illustrates the steady annual consumption in Norton from 1952 to 1960 and also the greater proportion of domestic, compared with trade (metered) consumption. Both market towns have several small industrial concerns on metered supplies which serve the surrounding agricultural areas. In Norton these include two bacon factories, a dairy, laundry, bakers, and manure works, the largest consumers being the bacon factories which consumed an average of 10·50 m.g.a., and 5·54 m.g.a. respectively between 1957 and 1961. The total consumption of trade (metered) supplies was 28 m.g. in 1952 and the same in 1960.

The four largest metered consumers in Driffield, i.e. sugar and flour mills, cattle market and hospital, each used over 1 m.g. in 1961.

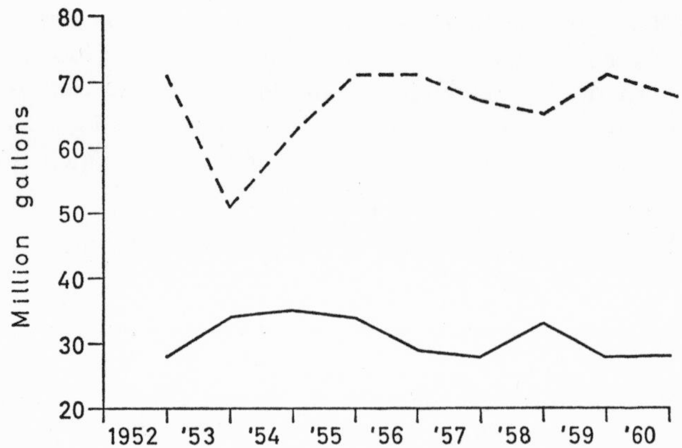

FIG. 10. ANNUAL CONSUMPTION OF WATER IN NORTON U.D., 1952–60.
Based on data supplied by Norton U.D.C.
Solid line = metered Broken line = non-metered (domestic supply)

Other metered supplies are provided for schools, the slaughterhouse, garages, railway station and sewage works. Several private boreholes still existed in 1962 when the Driffield Water Company was taken over by the E.Y. (W.A.) W.B.

In Table 15 it can be seen that Norton U.D.C. water undertaking estimated a surplus of 690,000 g.p.d. to requirements in 1985 from the Howe Hill borehole source, whereas Driffield Water Company, estimated neither a surplus nor a deficiency for 1985. Since the Company was bought by the E.Y. (W.A.) W.B., which had plans in 1962 to develop the Driffield R.D.C. Kilham borehole and possibly close down the Company's old Spellowgate source, plans have been formulated for the transfer of surplus water from one part of the Water Board's area to another where a deficiency might occur. This, therefore, alters the picture of estimated surplus or deficiency in Table 15.

WATER UTILIZATION IN THE RURAL DISTRICTS OF BEVERLEY, DRIFFIELD, POCKLINGTON, HOWDEN, NORTON AND DERWENT

The increase in consumption in rural districts both for domestic and agricultural supplies was discussed in Chapter 2 and again at the beginning of this section, when the average domestic consumption per head in 1949 was shown to be 29·9 g.p.d. (Table 13). The lack of piped water supply, water closets, and fixed baths in the Rural Districts in 1951 was shown to be particularly high in Driffield, Norton and Howden. The increase in population and consumption in all the Rural Districts between 1948 and 1961 was illustrated in Table 15. Not surprisingly, in largely agricultural areas, domestic consumption was in each case higher than trade consumption. It proved difficult to correlate data on rural consumption of water since records vary considerably from one water undertaking to another.

(*a*) *Beverley R.D.*

The numbers of houses in each parish, with the source of water supply on 31st December, 1960, is shown in Table 7. Table 24 shows the population and consumption of water increase between 1959 and 1961 in those parishes of Beverley R.D. within the statutory area of supply of Hull Corporation (which are supplied direct, not in bulk) while Table 15 shows the increase in population from 1948 to 1961 in the Beverley R.D.C. statutory area of supply. (The 1961 Census figure of 23,650 in Table 15 included the population of the whole Rural District).

TABLE 20

Financial Year	From Beverley Borough	From Driffield R.D.C.	From Howden R.D.C.	From South Cave Springs	Total Consumption
1950-51	85	19	66	23	193
1951-52	60	17	92	27	196
1952-53	87	17	117	15	236
1953-54	77	16	164	10	267
1954-55	67	10	154	29	260
1955-56	45	10	196	22	273
1956-57	27	9	207	20	263
1957-58	31	9	223	24	287
1958-59	27	11	215	32	285
1959-60	58	16	250	21	345*
1960-61	36	9	262	42	350

AVERAGE DAILY CONSUMPTION IN 1000 GALLONS IN BEVERLEY R.D.
1950-61 (FINANCIAL YEARS)

*Everthorpe Prison in operation.

The steady increase in consumption in the financial years from 1953/54 to 1960/61 can be seen in Figure 11(a). Total consumption during this period increased from 95·98 m.g.a. to 124·07 m.g.a. Table 20 illustrates the increase in daily average consumption from the four sources of water supply in financial years from 1950/51 to 1960/61. The total consumption figures given in Table 20 included water supplied from Hunsley reservoir to Hull Corporation at Riplingham.

(*b*) *Driffield R.D.*

The average consumption of 40·0 g.p.h.p.d. in 1948, shown in Table 15, was the highest in the East Riding and was most probably due to old, corroded water mains with a consequent high leakage rate, coupled with little or no waste detection in the R.D. In 1956 the average consumption for domestic purposes was 42·0 g.p.h.p.d., which was still high for a rural area, despite some improvement in the distribution mains and more efficient waste detection by night-sounding of service connections.

Figure 11(b) shows the quantity of water pumped into supply from each of the three borehole sources for those years from 1946 to 1960 where records are available. The quantity of water pumped from the Hutton Cranswick pumping station decreased from 129·45 m.g. in 1946/47 to 46·12 m.g. in 1959/60. Pumping from the Nafferton source reached a peak of 85·72 m.g. in 1953/54 but the pumping station was closed down in June, 1958. (No records were available for these two sources from 1949 to 1953). Figure 11(b) emphasises the importance of the new Kilham borehole source when the quantity of water pumped from this source increased from 126·35 m.g. in 1958/59 (the first full year of pumping) to 177·75 m.g. in 1959/60.

Table 21 summarises the consumption of water in Driffield R.D. in the calendar years 1959, 1960 and 1961. It can be seen that domestic consumption decreased between 1959 and 1961 but that the trade consumption remained fairly steady. These data are rather misleading, since in 1961 the metered consumption included approximately 900 farm meters which would not be classified as 'trade' consumption. As in all the Rural Districts, a very large proportion of the water used in Driffield is for agricultural supplies, and there is very little industry. For the financial year ending

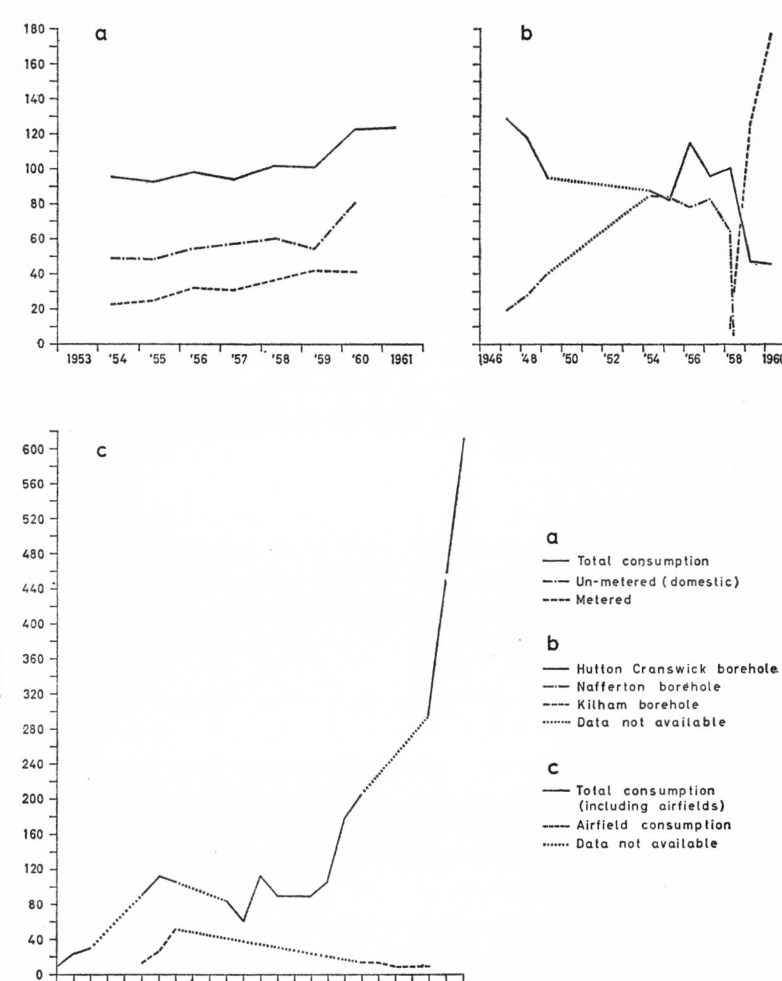

FIG. 11. ANNUAL WATER UTILISATION IN SELECTED RURAL DISTRICTS; (*a*) BEVERLEY R.D. (financial years), (*b*) DRIFFIELD R.D. (financial years), and (*c*) POCKLINGTON R.D.

Based on data supplied by R.D.C. Water undertakings and by John H. Haiste and Partners (consulting engineers).

TABLE 21

Consumption	1959	1960	1961
Domestic (unmetered)	389	310	290
Trade (metered)	240	260	260
Total	629	570	550
Daily average during peak week		m.g.d. 0·60	m.g.d. 0·58

CONSUMPTION OF WATER IN 1000 g.p.d. IN DRIFFIELD R.D., 1959-61

31st March, 1961, a total metered consumption of 88,233,000 g. was recorded, of which 50,653,000 g. was for agricultural supplies and 37,580,000 g. was for non-agricultural supplies, including an aerodrome at Kirkburn.

The reliable yield of the underground sources, i.e. the average daily yield maintainable over the worst drought period likely to be experienced, was estimated to be 2·4 m.g.d. in 1961 so that there was a considerable surplus over requirements. An estimated surplus of 570,000 g.p.d. over requirements by 1985 is shown in Table 15.

(*c*) *Pocklington R.D.*

The increase in annual consumption of metered and unmetered supplies in Pocklington R.D. from 10·47 m.g. in 1937 to 614·0 m.g. in 1961 can be seen in Fig. 11(c). There was a more rapid increase in consumption after the purchase of the Market Weighton Water Company in 1955 and the Pocklington Water Company in 1957, since the Council had to improve the distribution mains in both market towns, and provide for the increasing demand due to housing development. Although included in the total consumption in Figure 11(c), the consumption by airfields is also plotted separately from 1942, since it formed a substantial proportion of the total consumption during the war. Allerthorpe camp and Melbourne airfield closed in 1958 and Pocklington airfield closed in 1961.

At the end of 1959 there were approximately 1,180 meters in the area but of the total consumption in 1961 of 614·0 m.g., only 83·2 m.g. was metered supply and 530·84 m.g. was unmetered or domestic consumption. This consumption was by an estimated population of 13,906 on 31st December, 1961, but the 1961 Census figure given in Table 15 was 14,150.

As has been found typical in Rural Districts previously discussed, there is little industry in Pocklington R.D. apart from six or seven small factories on the disused Pocklington airfield, and three consumers of over 1 m.g.a. These three largest metered consumers were a poultry packing station in Pocklington, with an average consumption from 1958 to 1961 of 3 m.g.a., a dairy in Pocklington with a steady consumption, over the same period, of 1·68 m.g.a., and a plastics factory at Stamford Bridge with an average consumption of 1·42 m.g.a.

Although a severe strain was put on the Pocklington R.D. distribution system during the drought of 1959, a constant supply was maintained, and in contrast to Howden and Beverley, no restrictions were imposed. From 14th to 27th December, 1959, however 30,000 g.p.d. were obtained from Derwent R.D. via the emergency Elvington mains connection and 20,000 g.p.d. were obtained from Flaxton R.D. for six weeks via the emergency main connection at Stamford Bridge. This was the first occasion since the 1934 Regional Scheme had been initiated that a water supply was obtained from outside the statutory area of supply. As a consequence of the 1959 drought, a link main was installed at Market Weighton to extend the limits of the Market Weighton distribution, to feed Sancton and Cliffe villages and to relieve the demand on the North Newbald source of Howden R.D.C. A main from Londesborough springs was installed, to augment the available supply from the Warter source, to the Market Weighton area and Howden R.D. but unfortunately, in December 1959 the Market Weighton borehole and the Londesborough spring could not be used at the same time, although minimum yields of both are included in Table 22.

(*d*) *Howden R.D.*

Table 15 shows a comparatively small increase in population in Howden R.D. between 1948 and 1961 but Fig. 12(a) illustrates an increase in average consumption from 455,516 g.p.d. at the end of March, 1959 to 750,566 g.p.d. at the end of December, 1961. This latter figure, however, was rather higher than normal due to the effects of frost damage and burst mains. In 1956 the demand for domestic water supply was 25·8 g.p.h.p.d., which was similar to that of Pocklington R.D. to the north. This was a comparatively low consumption as much improvement in sanitary facilities in this agricultural district was still necessary. As previously mentioned, 30% of the households were without piped supplies at the 1951 Census, and in the early 1960's slow progress was being made in the installation of sewerage works for the villages in the Vale of York. A new sewage works for Howden town with an outfall to the River Ouse was not completed until 1963.

In 1961 there were approximately 1,000 farm meters, with an agricultural demand for approximately two gallons per acre per day where irrigation was not used. Very little 'trade' consumption existed in 1961, the largest consumer being a milk factory at Holme-on-Spalding Moor. In addition there were five brickyards, a creosote works, a flax mill at Howden, and one chemical works at Howdendyke which had an average consumption of 1 m.g.a. In 1956 the average 'trade' demand was 30,000 g.p.d., a large proportion of which was used by the milk factory.

Table 15 shows an estimated deficiency on requirements by 1985 of 250,000 g.p.d. The precarious state of water supplies in this area was very well displayed at the end of the dry summer of 1959. On 28th August, 1959, water shortage warning notices were posted throughout the Rural Districts of Howden and Beverley, prohibiting the use of hoses for gardens and car-washing. By November 1959, Howden R.D.C. were taking a bulk supply from Pocklington R.D.C. at Shiptonthorpe of about 150,000 g.p.d. to serve the northern part of their statutory area. By 7th December, 1959, there was a reduction in the yield of the South Cave springs to an extent never known in the history of the Local Scheme. Parts of Beverley R.D.C. had been without supply for 48 hours in that first week of December.

Pocklington R.D.C. could no longer supply so much water to Howden R.D.C. by 9th December, 1959 due to the low yields of the springs, and Holme-on-Spalding Moor reservoir was empty. Four parishes were without adequate supplies for more than 24 hours and the milk factory at Holme, employing 150 people, was within 30 minutes of complete stoppage. Howden R.D.C. were forced to divert water to this Holme area at an average rate of 130,000 g.p.d. from their North Newbald Pumping Station when the bores were falling fast. Thus all Howden R.D.C. efforts over the latter six months of 1959 to conserve supplies at North Newbald were nullified. By 10th December, 1959, the flow from Pocklington R.D.C. to Howden R.D.C. at both Shiptonthorpe and Harswell was further

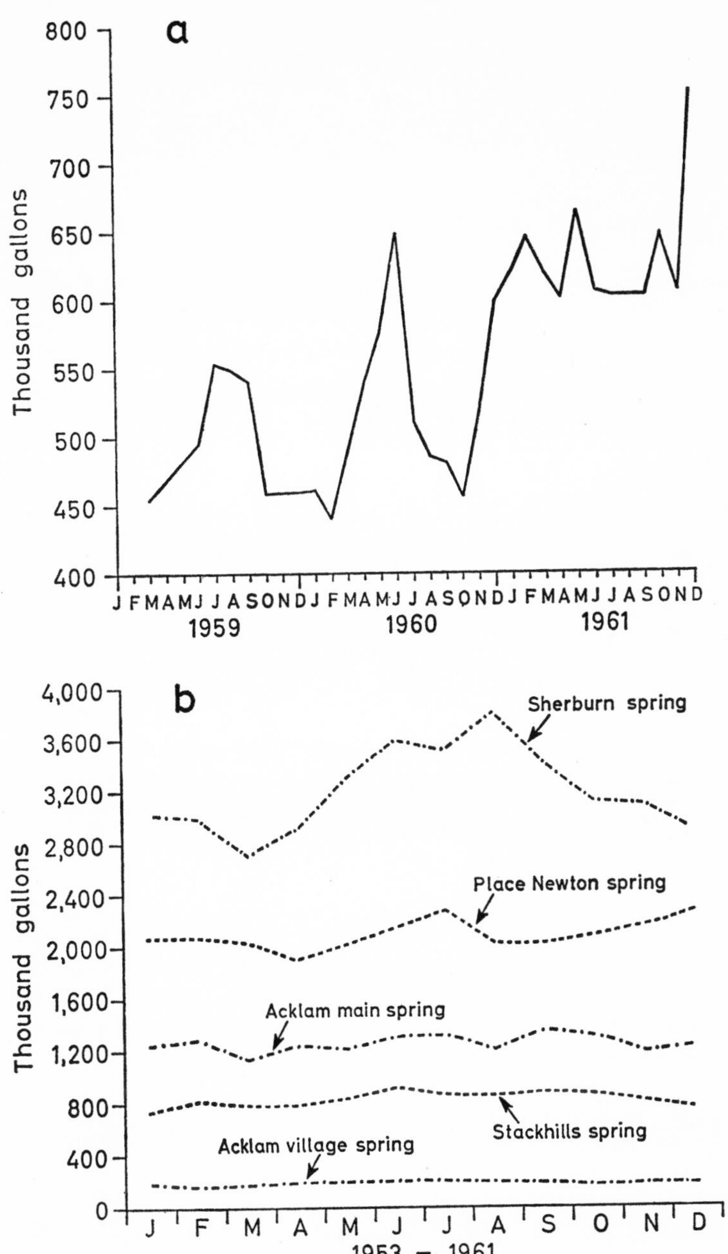

Fig. 12. Water Consumption in Two Rural Districts; (*a*) Howden R.D. (mean daily values) and (*b*) Norton R.D. (mean monthly values).
Based on data supplied by R.D.C. water undertakings.

reduced, the emergency supply to Holme from North Newbald had to be turned off, and the supply to the northern parishes of Howden R.D.C. was being watched from hour to hour. The Council had to increase the bulk supply from Goole Corporation and use the borehole source at North Newbald as carefully as possible until water levels began to rise again in January 1960.

A deficiency of 100,000 g.p.d. existed in Howden and Beverley in August 1959, so that the dry autumn (September and October) aggravated the water supply situation. Even though rainfall was above the average in November and December 1959 and January 1960, the water levels in the North Newbald bores were slow to recover because of the time taken for rainfall to reach the water table.

The total consumption in December 1959 in the Rural Districts of Howden, Beverley and Pocklington can be seen from Table 22 to be 1,420,000 g.p.d., while the minimum yield of the sources in the same month was only 1,340,000 g.p.d. (without bulk supplies from neighbouring authorities). Thus in December 1959, there was a deficiency in the three areas of 80,000 g.p.d.

TABLE 22

Statutory Undertakings	Consumption (1000 g.p.d.)	Sources of Water Supply	Minimum yields (1000 g.p.d.)
Howden R.D.	460	North Newbald boreholes	375
Beverley R.D.	310	South Cave Springs	3
Pocklington R.D.	650	R.D. Springs	450
		Pocklington springs	75
		Londesborough springs	80
		Market Weighton borehole	360
Total	1,420		1,340

CONSUMPTION, SOURCES AND MINIMUM YIELDS IN SELECTED RURAL DISTRICTS, DECEMBER, 1959

(*e*) *Norton R.D.*

The high domestic consumption per head in Norton R.D. (see Table 15) was second only to Driffield R.D. The agricultural nature of this district, with isolated farms and small villages, particularly in the higher Wolds, has led to a decline in population in these areas, although the overall population of Norton R.D. increased from 1948 to 1961.

Figure 12(b) shows the average monthly consumption from each spring source from 1953 to 1961, when adequate data were available. It can be seen that consumption from the Sherburn spring exceeded 3 m.g. in each month, except March, April, and December, and reached a peak of 3·80 m.g. in August. Consumption from the Place Newton spring exceeded 2 m.g. in every month except April, reaching a peak of 2·29 m.g. in July, while consumption from the Acklam main exceeded 1 m.g. in every month, reaching a maximum of 1·36 m.g. in September. Consumption from the Stackhills and Acklam village sources was very steady and lower than the previous three sources mentioned. A peak of 0·93 m.g. from Stackhills spring, and 0·21 m.g. from Acklam village spring both occurred in June.

All farms have metered supplies, and agricultural demand for water occupies the greatest proportion of consumption. The only sizeable industry is the Knapton silo, with an average consumption of 0·5 m.g. per week in 1962. One private supply, that of Lord Middleton's spring supply to his Birdsall Estate, still existed in 1962.

During 1961 the total monthly consumption varied between 11 and 12 m.g. In Table 15 it can be seen that Norton R.D.C. had estimated a surplus over requirements by 1985 of 560,000 g.p.d. with further development of the spring sources. Since the estimate was made, a changed situation was introduced when the water undertaking was superseded by the R. J.W.B. on 1st October, 1961. This Board was, in fact, already supplying the large demand for water by the Knapton silo from June 1961. Thus the Rural District can call on the Board's resources for future supply if it is found that no further development of the spring sources is possible in Norton R.D.

(*f*) *Derwent R.D.*

The total population of Derwent R.D. at the 1951 Census was 12,919 and Table 15 shows an increase to 13,760 at the 1961 Census. Total consumption, however, remained steady in 1960 and 1961 (see Table 23). Most of the industries are situated in Barlby parish, but in addition to these metered consumers, all farms have meters, so that the problem of separating 'trade' and 'agricultural' consumption in the metered consumption total remains insuperable. Market gardens in the Riccall area have meters, usually for domestic supply, and private borehole supplies for irrigation. Similarly, the largest industrial consumers in Barlby parish supplement their mains supply from a private borehole.

TABLE 23

Source of bulk supplies	Bulk supplies in 1000 g.p.d.	
	1960	1961
York Waterworks Company	158	156
Selby U.D.C.	278	283
Total	436	439
Metered consumption	189	190
Unmetered consumption	248	249
Daily average consumption during peak week	500	500

BULK SUPPLIES TO DERWENT R.D., 1960-61

Derwent R.D. remains apart from the rest of the county, for the water undertaking has been taken over by the York Waterworks Company in the northern part, and by the Pontefract, Goole and Selby Water Board in the southern part, so that all its water supply is now provided from outside the county.

WATER UTILISATION IN THE STATUTORY AREA OF THE WATER UNDERTAKING OF KINGSTON UPON HULL

A summary of the increasing population and total consumption of water in the statutory area of supply of Hull Corporation water undertaking for the period from 1918 to 1961 can be seen in Fig. 13 and from 1948 to 1961 in Table 15. The most rapid increase in consumption since 1945 has been in trade or metered supply. Waters (1949) reported an increase of 5% in trade consumption between 1935 and 1949, despite the hard water supplies. This trade supply included industrial concerns, some shops, hospitals, and market gardens, and the number of meters in Hull's 'city area' (i.e. supplied in detail) had reached approximately 6,000 in 1962. The largest metered consumers included several concerns in the chemical industry, which was developing rapidly at the Saltend oil terminal site to the east of the city. Eight 'trade' consumers in Hull in 1962 used an average of 1 m.g.d.

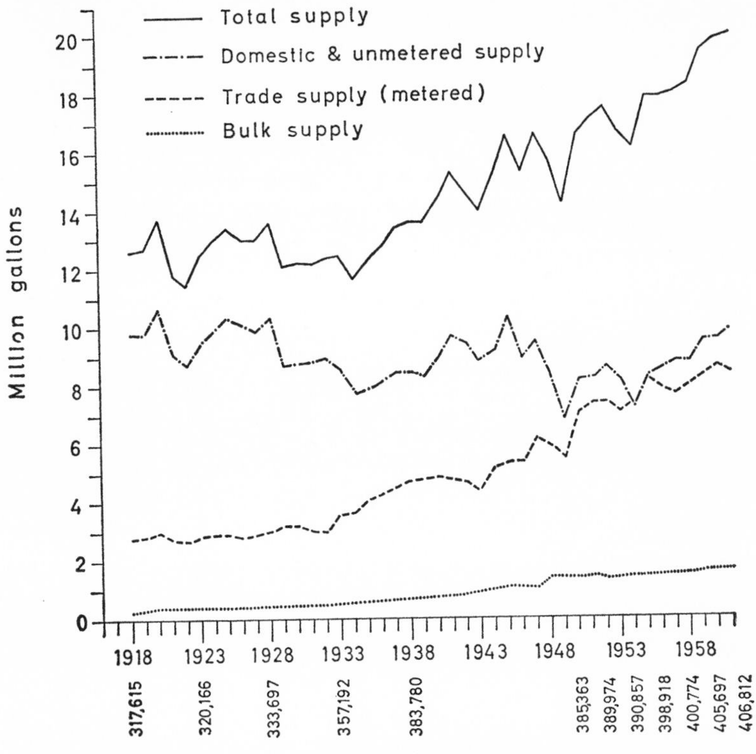

FIG. 13. WATER SUPPLIES IN THE STATUTORY AREA OF THE HULL CORPORATION WATER UNDERTAKING, 1918–61 (mean daily values).

Based on data supplied by the Corporation Water Department.

As previously mentioned, ten private boreholes in Hull in 1962 provided water, in addition to the metered mains supply, for three flour mills, a chocolate and confectionery firm, a manufacturer of boilers and radiators, a laundry, a dairy, the Gas Board and one refinery at Marfleet in the Hull city area. Two firms at Beverley

TABLE 24

Area supplied	1959			1960			1961		
	Population	Average Consumption (1000 g.p.d.)		Population	Average Consumption (1000 g.p.d.)		Population	Average Consumption (1000 g.p.d.)	
		Total	Average p.h.		Total	Average p.h.		Total	Average p.h.
(1) Direct:									
Hull City	301,800			302,400			303,268		
Holderness R.D.C. (95%)	20,020			19,513			19,342		
Haltemprice U.D.C. (2/3)	27,274			27,560			28,220		
Beverley R.D.C. (90%)	13,394			13,394			12,770		
Total	362,488	17,786	49·3	362,867	18,198	50·1	363,600	18,348	50·3
(2) In bulk:									
Haltemprice U.D.C. (1/3)	13,637		34·8	13,780	433	31·8	14,110	423	30·8
Hedon Corporation	2,250	70	31·5	2,250	79	35·0	2,338	90	39·9
Hornsea U.D.C.	5,670	216	38·6	5,760	222	38·8	5,760	227	39·3
Withernsea U.D.C.	4,980	165	33·1	4,980	170	34·1	4,980	191	38·3
Beverley Borough	15,660	695	44·5	16,062	728	46·6	16,024	747	46·5
Total	42,197	1,604	38·6	42,832	1,632	38·7	43,212	1,678	39·2

POPULATION SUPPLIED AND AVERAGE DAILY CONSUMPTION OF WATER IN HULL CORPORATION WATER DEPARTMENT STATUTORY AREA 1959-61 making fertilizers had private borehole supplies. Cottingham Drain provided a private source for iron founders and paper manufacturers, the Foredyke Stream for the Gas Board, and the Barmston Drain for a tannery, stone-sawing firm, shipyard, and for cooling purposes by the Central Electricity Generating Board at Sculcoates Power Station. This latter abstraction for cooling purposes had decreased from 7,496 m.g. between 1st April, 1952 and 31st March, 1953 (an average of 20·5 m.g.d.) to 2,812 m.g. from 1st April, 1963 and 31st March, 1964 (an average of 7·7 m.g.d.). All these private abstractions from surface waters in Hull were by agreement with the then Hull and East Yorkshire R.B.

In Figure 13 the increase in demand for bulk supplies can be seen to be a steady one, but the domestic and unmetered supplies fluctuated between 1918 and 1961, especially after the war in 1945, and only showed a steady increase after 1955. Waste detection methods and pleas for economies in water consumption from 1945 up to this date were discussed earlier. The actual quantities of water consumed in the Corporation's statutory area in the years 1959 to 1961 can be seen in Tables 24 and 25.

TABLE 25

Year	1959	1960	1961
Population supplied direct and to bulk supply areas	404,685	405,699	406,812
Bulk supply	1,604	1,632	1,678
Domestic supply (unmetered)	9,490	9,612	9,947
Trade supply (metered)	8,262	8,555	8,378
Sewers supply	0·033	0·030	0·028
Shipping supply	0·001	0·001	—
Total	19·390	19·830	20·026

SUMMARY OF AVERAGE DAILY CONSUMPTION IN M.G. IN HULL CORPORATION WATER DEPARTMENT STATUTORY AREA, 1959-61

The very small consumption under the heading "shipping" in Table 25 was a small supply to the dock area which was discontinued in 1961. The consumption under 'sewers' constituted the quantity of water used to periodically flush out the city's sewers. Total consumption in the statutory area increased in 1959 when water was first pumped from the Tophill Low Pumping Station in the September quarter. Before this date consumption had been kept down artificially (as previous mentioned) to between 18 and 20 m.g.d. In 1962 the Corporation supplied between 24 and 26 m.g.d. and the maximum capacity which could be supplied with the existing pumping capacity and size of mains was approximately 30 m.g.d. The maximum capacity of the existing pumping stations in 1962 was 10 m.g.d. at Dunswell and Cottingham, 8 m.g.d. at Springhead, and 12 m.g.d. at Tophill Low. Thus a total of 40 m.g.d. was available in 1962, but inadequate main size and limited pumping capacity precluded this supply being given.

In January 1964, the Corporation Water Committee decided to proceed with a new water main to ensure an adequate supply for the increasing demand in west Hull. This main would be laid from Keldgate reservoir, Cottingham, to Hessle Road, Hull, in order to relieve the load on Springhead Pumping Station which was already supplying Hessle, Anlaby, Willerby, Ferriby and Brough. The Water Engineer emphasised that due to increasing demands, and particularly during drought conditions, the rapidly developing West Hull area would not receive adequate supplies, in spite of the fact that the Department's water resources were sufficient for all purposes.

CHAPTER 4

CONCLUSIONS AND PROSPECT

IN 1956, Vail commented on the difficulty of knowing an exact figure for average consumption, especially in the Rural Districts. Table 15 summarises the population and water supply position in the East Riding between 1948 and 1961. Increases in population and consumption during this period were rapid in Hull's statutory area of supply, which included the seaside resorts of Hornsea and Withernsea, and in the other two resorts of Filey and Bridlington, but remained fairly steady in the market towns of Driffield and Norton. Population increase was generally small in the Rural Districts, with a decline in population recorded in Norton R.D. between 1955 and 1961. Nevertheless, the consumption of water in these areas increased due to improvement in housing and sanitation and the extension of mains water supply.

It was noted earlier (p. 68) that Vail considered the sources of water being exploited in the county in 1956 would meet foreseeable demand for 30 years, but only by passing local surpluses to other needy areas. His estimates of 35 g.p.h.p.d. for domestic supplies in urban areas and 30 g.p.h.p.d. for domestic supplies in rural areas in 1985, although admittedly for average consumption, were very conservative, particularly when these figures are compared with the average consumption of 40 g.p.h.p.d. in Driffield R.D. in 1948, which had increased to 42 g.p.h.p.d. in 1956.

The urban areas of Beverley, Hedon, Haltemprice, Hornsea and Withernsea are shown in Table 15 to have estimated deficiencies in their supplies by 1985, all of which will have to be met by the statutory Water Undertaking of Hull Corporation Water Department. It was noted that a deficiency of 80,000 g.p.d. was assessed at the end of 1959 for the Rural Districts of Beverley, Howden and Pocklington. Any future deficiency is now the responsibility of the E.Y. (W.A.) W.B., which has already developed a new borehole source at Etton to supply areas of need in Beverley and Howden Rural Districts.

Vail, in the last regional assessment of water supplies to be carried out for the whole county, advocated amalgamation of water undertakings (which has since taken place) and considered it was essential for water supplies to be planned on an areal basis, so that suitable sources could be used to the best advantage—a view which is now postulated by the Water Resources Board. He noted that while ample water resources existed for domestic, agricultural and industrial requirements in the county up to 1985, few sources of 15 m.g.d. or more existed to supply any rapid increase in demand. The growth of irrigation in the county has been mentioned, and also the rapid growth in the Hull area with possible further expansion, particularly if the proposed Humber bridge is constructed to open up the Humberside region for further industrial development. Both of these factors would mean a rapidly increasing demand for water. It was noted in Chapter 2 that Hull Corporation Water Department had surveyed the county for possible reservoir sites and found that Farndale and the two adjacent valleys in the North Riding were the only possible sites. Several sites existed in the East Riding where groundwater supplies of the order of three or four m.g.d. could be obtained, but river intakes seemed to provide the chief hope for large supplies.

The River Hull is being exploited to near maximum by Hull Corporation in the Tophill Low abstraction. The River Ouse provides water supplies for York and surrounding areas from an intake at Acomb. Below York the river is polluted by sewage from York and Selby and from the Rivers Wharfe, Aire, Don and Trent, and the pollution and sediment load in the Humber precludes its use as a source of water, as already mentioned. Thus the River Derwent remains the only possible major additional source of water supply to the county. Vail suggested an abstraction scheme at Sutton on the Derwent to supply Hull, as the intake site would be much nearer than Farndale. The river has a sizeable dry weather flow and is largely spring-fed, so that the water would be similar in quality to the existing sources of Hull Corporation. Vail suggested that of an abstraction of 25 m.g.d., 5 m.g.d. could be pumped to Hull while 20 m.g.d. could be pumped to Sheffield, where a shortage of water also existed.

The Yorkshire Derwent Scheme was first promoted by Sheffield Corporation Water Department in 1957, on quite different terms from those put forward by Vail in 1956. The first stage of the scheme was to abstract 15 m.g.d. from the River Derwent near Elvington, approximately six miles east of York, filter and treat the water at the intake site, and pump it through a 37-mile aqueduct to Sheffield as shown in Figure 14. By the terms of the Sheffield Water Order, 1961, 3·9 m.g.d. would be available for Barnsley at Ringstone Hill, 2·0 m.g.d. would be available for Rotherham and 7·8 m.g.d. for Sheffield from Hoober reservoir. Hull was not included in the scheme. The Derwent was chosen as the only major new source of water available to the West Riding of Yorkshire where an already large demand for water was steadily increasing. Treatment at the

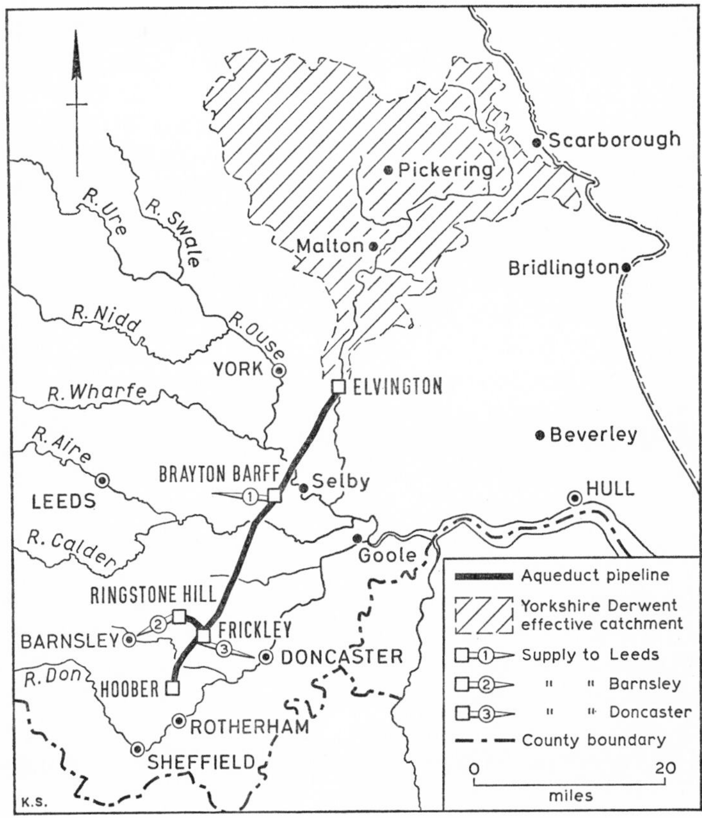

Fig. 14. Simplified Map of the Yorkshire Derwent Scheme. Based on data supplied by Sheffield Corporation Waterworks.

intake would include softening of the water to a standard similar to that of the upland Pennine soft water which provided Sheffield's existing supply. The intake site was chosen where there would be minimum interference to the freshwater regime of the river, where water could be abstracted during all flow conditions, where silting could be avoided, and where suitable ground existed for the pumping station, treatment works and houses.

As a result of changing attitudes in river management, it is now felt that peak floods, especially in the Derwent, should be conserved in some way, instead of being rushed to the sea as soon as possible. In preliminary discussions between Sheffield Corporation and the former Y.O.R.B. on the abstraction rate from the River Derwent at Elvington, the existing low flow records for the period 1939 to 1958, computed from the original Stamford Bridge weir data, formed the basis of the discussions. The initial abstraction was to be only 15 m.g.d. When planning the pumping station at Elvington, treatment works and pipeline size, the designs were based upon an increasing supply derived from the trends of demand of the water undertakings in the West Riding. The Sheffield Water Department estimated that, with proper reservoiring in the head-waters, the river might be made to yield a constant supply of perhaps 100 m.g.d. It is interesting to note this forward planning, but in fact, in 1964 the Y.O.R.B. granted an abstraction rate of 25 m.g.d. (46·49 cusecs) and this was the maximum abstraction rate permitted without conservation works on the river, whereby the flow can be artificially increased. 25 m.g.d. would be an insignificant proportion of flood flows, but it would be a significant proportion of the fourteen day minimum flows shown in Table 26. It is likely that a regulating reservoir for the River Derwent will be constructed in Farndale where Hull Corporation has statutory powers to build a reservoir. Thus an increased abstraction rate could be agreed by the Y.O.H.R.A. for the West Riding towns and it seems likely that Hull Corporation Water Department will be included in any future expansion of the Yorkshire Derwent Scheme (The Farndale regulating reservoir scheme was, in fact, approved by the Y.O.H.R.A., on the above basis, in March 1968). The first water from Elvington was delivered to Sheffield on 4th December, 1964, but the Yorkshire Derwent Scheme was officially opened at Elvington pumping station on 10th September, 1965.

It is interesting to note that with the abstraction of up to 25 m.g.d. from the River Derwent by the West Riding towns previously mentioned, all of which have a rapidly increasing demand for water, the last remaining major source of water for the future demand of the East Riding has been lost insofar as its exclusive use is concerned. It was previously noted that Vail recommended the development of the Derwent by Hull Corporation in 1958. It is evident, therefore, that with the recent approval of the Farndale regulating reservoir and the incorporation of Hull into the Yorkshire Derwent scheme, completion of the scheme is likely within the next decade, or at least by 1985.

TABLE 26

Year	Discharge	
	m.g.d.	cusecs
1956	119·8	222·8
1952	110·0	204·6
1957	100·5	186·9
1954	100·5	186·9
1950	100·5	186·9
1939	96·74	179·9
1940	85·78	159·5
1941	82·24	153·0
1953	78·74	146·4
1948	78·74	146·4
1945	78·74	146·4
1944	71·89	133·7
1942	71·89	133·7
1955	60·43	112·4
1949	58·83	109·4

FOURTEEN DAY MINIMUM FLOWS IN RIVER DERWENT AT STAMFORD BRIDGE

A major factor to emerge from this survey has been the incompleteness of data within the statutory water undertakings in the county, making it impossible to assess demands for domestic, industrial, and agricultural consumption. Basic hydrological data, however, are also inadequate and since under the terms of the 1963 Water Resources Act, the responsibility for conservation of water resources lies with the river authority, the Y.O.H.R.A. are now formulating their hydrometric scheme to solve this hydrological problem. Full co-operation in the East Riding is necessary between the River Authority and the two major statutory water undertakings, namely Hull Corporation and the East Yorkshire (Wolds Area) Water Board in order to solve the other problem of inadequate data on consumption of water and future demand. Existing resources must be utilised to their full extent and conserved wherever possible, so that resources should be sufficient within the chalk aquifer and the Rivers Derwent and Hull to meet all foreseeable demands up to the year 2,000.

References

Board of Trade. 1958. Industry and Industrial Development in Lincolnshire and the East Riding, *Board of Trade Journal*, vol. 175.

Boulton, A. G. 1962. The bearing of hydrology on water conservation, *River Boards' Assoc. Yearbook*, 1962.

Buchan, S. 1955. Artificial replenishment of aquifers, *J. Inst. Water Eng.* vol. 9.

Cole, E. M. 1894. Notices of Wetwang, *Trans. East Riding Antiquarian Soc.* vol. II.

East Riding County Council. 1952. *County Development Plan, Report of Survey*, The County Council, Beverley.

Fairbank, A. C. 1923. Report to Howden R.D.C. water undertaking by Fairbank and Son, Consulting Engineers, York.

Fox-Strangways, C. 1892. The Jurassic rocks of Yorkshire, *Mem. Geol. Survey.*

Green, C. 1949. Water resources of the Yorkshire chalk, Address to Hull Geological Soc.

Haiste, J. H. 1945. Report on the co-ordination of water supplies to the Beverley, Howden and Pocklington Rural District Councils by J. H. Haiste and Partners, Consulting Engineers, Leeds.

Haiste, J. H. 1959. Report on water consumption in the Rural Districts of Beverley, Howden and Pocklington by J. H. Haiste and Partners, Consulting Engineers, Leeds.

Harris, A. 1961. *The Rural Landscape of the East Riding of Yorkshire, 1700-1850*, Hull Univ. Press.

Head, G. 1836. Home tour through the manufacturing districts of England in 1835.

Hull Corporation, 1960. Brief description of the River Hull Abstraction Scheme (City and County of Kingston upon Hull) September, 1960.

Isaac, P. C. G. 1965. Water, waste and wealth, *Water and Wat. Eng.*, vol. 69.

Jones, T. H. 1955. The water supply of Kingston upon Hull from 1292 to 1954 and the future sources of supply, *J. Roy. Sanitary Inst.* vol. 75.

Lapworth, H. 1933. East Riding water supplies, A hydro-geological survey and waterworks survey report by H. Lapworth Partners Consulting Engineers, London.

LEATHAM, I. 1794. *General View of the agriculture of the East Riding of Yorkshire*, Balmer, London.

M.A.A.F. 1954. The calculation of irrigation need, *M.A.A.F. Tech.* Bull. 4. H.M.S.O.

M.A.A.F. 1962. Irrigation, *M.A.A.F. Bull.* 138 (3rd ed.) H.M.S.O.

MacMahon, K. A. 1958. Beverley Corporation Minute Book (1707-1835), *Yorks. Arch. Soc. Rec. Series*, vol. CXXII.

MARSHALL, W. 1796. *The rural economy of Yorkshire, Vol. I* (2nd Ed.) Nicol, London.

MAYOH, K. L. 1961. *A Comparative study of resorts on the coast of Holderness* Unpublished M.A. Thesis, University of Hull.

MOORE, D. 1949. Communication to Driffield R.D.C. from D. Moore, Esq., Consulting Engineer, Scarborough.

NATURAL RESOURCES (Technical) COMMITTEE, 1962. Irrigation in Great Britain, *Nat. Res. Tech. Cttee. Rept.*, H.M.S.O.

OAKLEY, K. P., BUSH and TOOMBS, 1944. Water supply from underground sources of East Yorkshire and North Lincolnshire, *Geol. Surv. Wartime Pamphlet* No. 12, Parts I and II.

REGISTRAR-GENERAL, 1964. *Census of England and Wales, 1961: Yorkshire East Riding County Report.* H.M.S.O.

REID, C. 1885. The geology of Holderness, *Mem. Geol. Surv.*, 1885.

SHEAHAN, J. J. 1865. *History of the town and port of Kingston-upon-Hull.* J. Green, Beverley.

SILCOCK, E. J. 1922. Report to Hornsea, U.D.C. Waterworks Cttee. by E. J. Silcock, Engineer and Surveyor, Leeds.

VAIL, A. R. 1956. *Yorkshire (East and North Ridings) Water Survey*, Ministry of Housing and Local Government, H.M.S.O.

VERSEY, H. C. 1948. The structure of East Yorkshire and North Lincolnshire, *Proc. Yorks. Geol. Soc.* vol. 27.

VERSEY, H. C. 1949. The hydrology of the East Riding of Yorkshire, *Proc. Yorks. Geol. Soc.* vol. 27.

WATER RESOURCES BOARD, 1966. Water supplies in south east England, *Water Resources Board Report*, H.M.S.O.

WATERS, A. H. S. 1949. Report on the East Riding Water Authorities.

YOUNG, A. 1770. *A six months' tour through the north of England, Vol. II.* Strahan, London.